The Complete Soup Cookbook

Quick & Tasty Recipes for Every Season | Make Wonderful Dishes with Simple Ingredients Suitable for Every Diet - Exclusive Bonus Included

Copyright Notice

Disclaimer

The recipes and suggestions in *The Complete Soup Cookbook* are for informational and educational purposes only. While every effort has been made to ensure the accuracy and safety of the information provided, the author and publisher are not responsible for any adverse effects or consequences resulting from the use of any recipes, instructions, or suggestions in this book.

All nutritional values provided are approximate and may vary depending on specific ingredients and preparation methods. Readers are encouraged to consult their doctor or a licensed dietitian before making any significant dietary changes, especially if they have allergies, medical conditions, or dietary restrictions.

The inclusion of any brands, products, or companies in this book is not an endorsement or recommendation. All trademarks and registered trademarks are the property of their respective owners.

By using this book, you agree to take full responsibility for your own health and actions. The author and publisher shall not be held liable for any damages arising from the use or misuse of the information contained in this book.

Table of Contents

How to Use This Book

Welcome to your new favorite cookbook! We created this book with **you** in mind, because we know how important it is to make cooking simple, fun, and stress-free. Whether you're planning a quiet night in or hosting a crowd, we've packed this book with hundreds of soups that are easy to find, easy to follow, and absolutely delicious.

We've thought of everything to make this your go-to guide for every season and occasion. From cozy winter stews to refreshing summer gazpachos, you'll find recipes that fit perfectly with what you need—and we'll help you every step of the way.

Finding the Right Recipe Made Easy

We know you don't have time to waste flipping through pages trying to find the perfect dish. That's why we've organized this book to make it as easy as possible to find what you need:

- **Seasonal Chapters**: Recipes are divided into Spring, Summer, Fall, and Winter, so you can cook with the freshest ingredients available.
- **By Main Ingredient**: Within each season, you'll find soups grouped by their main ingredient, like tomatoes, potatoes, or asparagus. This makes it super easy to use what you already have in your kitchen.

What Makes This Book Special?

This isn't just another cookbook—it's a tool to help you feel confident and inspired in the kitchen. Here's what you'll love:

- **Simple Recipes**: Every recipe has step-by-step instructions that are clear and easy to follow. Even if you're a beginner, you've got this!
- **Quick Adjustments**: Recipes are written for one serving, with tips on how to scale up for family meals or parties. No math headaches here!
- **Seasonal Tips**: Bonus sections guide you on how to choose the freshest ingredients, substitute off-season produce, and store leftovers like a pro.
- **Exclusive Bonuses**: Discover secret family favorites and party-worthy soups that will wow your guests.

Getting Started

1. **Flip to the Current Season**: Use the seasonal chapters to find soups that highlight the freshest produce available right now.
   - Example: Got some fresh zucchini in the summer? Try Zucchini and Basil Soup or Sweet Corn and Jalapeño Chowder.
2. **Search by Ingredient**: Use the index to find recipes based on what's in your fridge or pantry. Have some kale? You'll find comforting recipes like Rustic Potato and Kale Stew.
3. **Explore Something New**: Don't miss the bonus recipes, party soups, and seasonal pairing ideas to keep your kitchen exciting and creative.

We Care About Your Cooking Journey

We know that cooking can sometimes feel overwhelming. That's why we've made this book simple, clear, and full of love. It's not just about the recipes—it's about making your time in the kitchen something you look forward to. Whether you're trying a new soup or sticking with a classic, we're here to make sure every dish feels like a success. So grab a spoon, pick a recipe, and let's create something wonderful together. This isn't just a cookbook—it's your new cooking companion. We're so happy to be part of your journey. Let's get started!

Winter: Warm and Comforting
Potatoes

Creamy Potato and Leek Soup

Serves: 1 | Prep Time: 10 mins | Cook Time: 25 mins

Ingredients

- **Potatoes**: ½ cup (peeled and diced)
- **Leek**: ½ medium (sliced, white and light green parts only)
- **Garlic**: 1 clove (minced)
- **Olive oil**: 1 teaspoon
- **Vegetable broth**: 1¼ cups
- **Whole milk or cream**: ¼ cup
- **Salt and black pepper**: To taste
- **Optional garnish**: Chopped chives

Instructions

1. **Sauté Aromatics**: Heat **olive oil** in a pot over medium heat. Add **leeks** and **garlic**, cooking for 3–4 minutes until softened.
2. **Simmer the Soup**: Add **potatoes** and **vegetable broth**. Simmer for 15–20 minutes until the potatoes are tender.
3. **Blend and Add Milk**: Blend the soup until smooth. Stir in **milk or cream** and heat gently without boiling.
4. **Season and Serve**: Adjust seasoning with **salt** and **pepper**. Garnish with chopped **chives**.

Tips and Tricks

- For a deeper flavor, sauté the leeks until lightly caramelized.
- Add a splash of white wine before simmering for a sophisticated touch.

Loaded Baked Potato Soup

Serves: 1 | Prep Time: 15 mins | Cook Time: 30 mins

Ingredients

- **Potatoes**: ½ cup (peeled and diced)
- **Bacon**: 1 slice (chopped)
- **Onion**: ¼ medium (chopped)
- **Garlic**: 1 clove (minced)
- **Vegetable broth**: 1¼ cups
- **Whole milk or cream**: ¼ cup
- **Cheddar cheese**: 2 tablespoons (shredded)
- **Salt and black pepper**: To taste
- **Optional garnish**: Sour cream and green onions

Instructions

1. **Cook the Bacon**: In a pot, cook **bacon** until crispy. Remove and set aside.
2. **Sauté the Onion**: In the bacon drippings, sauté **onion** and **garlic** for 3–4 minutes.
3. **Simmer the Soup**: Add **potatoes** and **vegetable broth**, simmering for 15–20 minutes until the potatoes are tender.
4. **Blend and Add Milk**: Blend half the soup for a creamy texture while leaving chunks intact. Stir in **milk** and **cheddar cheese**.
5. **Season and Serve**: Adjust seasoning and garnish with sour cream, green onions, and crispy bacon.

Tips and Tricks

- Use smoked bacon for an extra flavor boost.
- Add a dash of smoked paprika for a subtly smoky taste.

Rustic Potato and Bacon Chowder

Serves: 1 | Prep Time: 10 mins | Cook Time: 30 mins

Ingredients

- **Potatoes**: ½ cup (peeled and diced)
- **Bacon**: 1 slice (chopped)
- **Onion**: ¼ medium (chopped)
- **Garlic**: 1 clove (minced)
- **Vegetable broth**: 1¼ cups
- **Whole milk or cream**: ¼ cup
- **Thyme**: ¼ teaspoon (fresh or dried)
- **Salt and black pepper**: To taste
- **Optional garnish**: Fresh thyme sprig

Instructions

1. **Cook the Bacon**: In a pot, cook **bacon** until crispy. Remove and set aside.
2. **Sauté the Onion**: In the bacon drippings, sauté **onion**, **garlic**, and **thyme** for 3–4 minutes.
3. **Simmer the Soup**: Add **potatoes** and **vegetable broth**. Simmer for 20 minutes until the potatoes are tender.
4. **Blend and Add Milk**: Partially blend the soup for a creamy yet rustic texture. Stir in **milk** and season with **salt** and **pepper**.
5. **Serve and Garnish**: Garnish with crispy bacon and a sprig of fresh thyme.

Tips and Tricks

- For added heartiness, stir in a handful of corn or peas before serving.
- Serve with crusty bread to soak up the delicious broth.

Potato and Cheddar Soup

Serves: 1 | Prep Time: 10 mins | Cook Time: 25 mins

Ingredients

- **Potatoes**: ½ cup (peeled and diced)
- **Cheddar cheese**: ¼ cup (shredded)
- **Onion**: ¼ medium (chopped)
- **Garlic**: 1 clove (minced)
- **Vegetable broth**: 1¼ cups
- **Whole milk or cream**: ¼ cup
- **Paprika**: ¼ teaspoon
- **Salt and black pepper**: To taste
- **Optional garnish**: Chives and additional shredded cheese

Instructions

1. **Sauté Aromatics**: Heat **olive oil** in a pot. Add **onion** and **garlic**, cooking for 3 minutes.
2. **Simmer the Soup**: Add **potatoes** and **vegetable broth**, and simmer for 15–20 minutes until the potatoes are tender.
3. **Blend and Add Cheese**: Blend the soup until smooth. Stir in **milk**, **cheddar cheese**, and **paprika**, heating gently until the cheese melts.
4. **Season and Serve**: Adjust seasoning with **salt** and **pepper**. Garnish with additional shredded cheese and chives.

Tips and Tricks

- For a smoky kick, use smoked cheddar or add a pinch of smoked paprika.
- Make it extra indulgent by topping with crispy bacon bits.

Benefits of Potato Soups

Benefit	Why It's Great
Warmth and Comfort	Keeps you cozy and warm during cold winter days.
Energy Boost	Potatoes give you long-lasting energy from their healthy carbs.
Rich in Potassium	Helps muscles and nerves work well, and supports healthy blood pressure.
Affordable and Easy	Potatoes are cheap, easy to find, and perfect for winter meals.
Immune System Support	Paired with garlic and onions, potato soup helps fight off colds and flu.
Hydrates Your Body	The broth in soup keeps you hydrated in dry winter air.
Gentle on Your Stomach	Easy to digest and soothing, even when you don't feel 100%.
Packed with Nutrients	Add other winter veggies like carrots or leeks for extra vitamins.
Customizable Flavors	Works with winter spices like rosemary, thyme, or paprika for seasonal goodness.
Boosts Your Mood	A warm bowl of soup can make you feel happy and relaxed on gloomy days.

Tip: Add garnishes like shredded cheese or chives to make it look extra special!

Cauliflower

Roasted Cauliflower Soup with Garlic

Serves: 1 | Prep Time: 10 mins | Cook Time: 30 mins

Ingredients

- **Cauliflower florets**: 1 cup
- **Garlic**: 1 clove (whole)
- **Onion**: ¼ medium (chopped)
- **Olive oil**: 1 teaspoon
- **Vegetable broth**: 1¼ cups
- **Salt and black pepper**: To taste
- **Optional garnish**: Croutons or a drizzle of olive oil

Instructions

1. **Roast the Cauliflower**: Preheat oven to 400°F (200°C). Toss **cauliflower** and **garlic** with **olive oil**, season with **salt** and **pepper**, and roast for 20 minutes until golden.
2. **Sauté the Onion**: Heat a small pot and sauté **onion** in a little oil for 3 minutes.
3. **Combine and Simmer**: Add the roasted **cauliflower** and **garlic** to the pot with **vegetable broth**. Simmer for 10 minutes.
4. **Blend and Serve**: Blend the soup until smooth. Adjust seasoning with **salt** and **pepper**. Garnish with croutons or a drizzle of olive oil.

Tips and Tricks

- Add a squeeze of lemon juice for brightness.
- For a nuttier flavor, roast the cauliflower until deeply golden.

Cauliflower and Cheddar Chowder

Serves: 1 | Prep Time: 10 mins | Cook Time: 25 mins

Ingredients

- **Cauliflower florets**: 1 cup (chopped)
- **Potato**: ¼ cup (diced)
- **Onion**: ¼ medium (chopped)
- **Garlic**: 1 clove (minced)
- **Cheddar cheese**: ¼ cup (shredded)
- **Vegetable broth**: 1 cup
- **Whole milk or cream**: ¼ cup
- **Salt and black pepper**: To taste
- **Optional garnish**: Additional shredded cheese

Instructions

1. **Sauté Aromatics**: Heat **olive oil** in a pot over medium heat. Add **onion** and **garlic**, cooking for 3 minutes.
2. **Cook Vegetables**: Add **cauliflower**, **potato**, and **vegetable broth**, simmering for 15 minutes until tender.
3. **Blend and Add Cheese**: Blend the soup until smooth. Stir in **milk** and **cheddar cheese**, heating gently until the cheese melts.
4. **Season and Serve**: Adjust seasoning with **salt** and **pepper**. Garnish with extra cheese if desired.

Tips and Tricks

- For a richer flavor, use aged cheddar.
- Add a dash of mustard for a tangy kick.

Spicy Cauliflower and Coconut Soup

Serves: 1 | Prep Time: 10 mins | Cook Time: 25 mins

Ingredients

- **Cauliflower florets**: 1 cup
- **Garlic**: 1 clove (minced)
- **Ginger**: ½ teaspoon (grated)
- **Red chili flakes**: ¼ teaspoon (optional)
- **Coconut milk**: ½ cup
- **Vegetable broth**: 1 cup
- **Olive oil**: 1 teaspoon
- **Salt and black pepper**: To taste
- **Optional garnish**: Fresh cilantro

Instructions

1. **Sauté Aromatics**: Heat **olive oil** in a pot. Add **garlic**, **ginger**, and **chili flakes**, cooking for 1–2 minutes.
2. **Cook Cauliflower**: Add **cauliflower** and stir well. Cook for 5 minutes.
3. **Simmer the Soup**: Add **coconut milk** and **vegetable broth**, simmering for 15 minutes until the cauliflower is tender.
4. **Blend and Serve**: Blend the soup until smooth. Adjust seasoning and garnish with fresh cilantro.

Tips and Tricks

- Use roasted cauliflower for an extra smoky flavor.
- Adjust the spice level by adding more or less chili flakes.

Cauliflower and Truffle Soup

Serves: 1 | Prep Time: 10 mins | Cook Time: 25 mins

Ingredients

- **Cauliflower florets**: 1 cup
- **Onion**: ¼ medium (chopped)
- **Garlic**: 1 clove (minced)
- **Truffle oil**: ½ teaspoon
- **Vegetable broth**: 1 cup
- **Whole milk or cream**: ¼ cup
- **Salt and black pepper**: To taste
- **Optional garnish**: Drizzle of truffle oil or thin truffle slices

Instructions

1. **Sauté Aromatics**: Heat **olive oil** in a pot. Add **onion** and **garlic**, cooking for 3 minutes.
2. **Cook Cauliflower**: Add **cauliflower** and **vegetable broth**, simmering for 15 minutes until the cauliflower is tender.
3. **Blend and Add Cream**: Blend the soup until smooth. Stir in **milk or cream** and drizzle with **truffle oil**.
4. **Season and Serve**: Adjust seasoning with **salt** and **pepper**. Garnish with a touch of truffle oil.

Tips and Tricks

- Pair with crusty bread for an elegant appetizer.
- Use high-quality truffle oil for the best flavor.

Benefits of Cauliflower Soups

Benefit	Why It's Great
Warmth and Comfort	A steaming bowl of cauliflower soup keeps you warm during chilly days.
Rich in Vitamins	Cauliflower is high in vitamin C, boosting your immunity in cold weather.
Low in Calories	A healthy and light option for hearty winter meals.
Supports Digestion	High fiber content helps keep your digestive system happy and healthy.
Affordable and Seasonal	Cauliflower is often cheaper and fresher in winter, making it a great choice.
Hydration in Dry Air	Soups keep you hydrated during the dry winter months.
Customizable Flavors	Pairs well with winter spices like nutmeg, turmeric, and black pepper for variety.
Great for Weight Goals	Low-carb and filling, it's perfect for staying healthy and satisfied.
Supports Bone Health	Contains calcium and vitamin K, important for strong bones in winter months.
Mood Booster	Creamy cauliflower soup is soothing and uplifting during dreary winter days.

Tip: Garnish with roasted cauliflower florets or toasted nuts for extra texture and flavor!

Kale

Kale and Sausage Stew

Serves: 1 | Prep Time: 10 mins | Cook Time: 30 mins

Ingredients

- **Kale**: 1 cup (chopped, stems removed)
- **Sausage**: 1 small link (sliced)
- **Potato**: ½ cup (diced)
- **Onion**: ¼ medium (chopped)
- **Garlic**: 1 clove (minced)
- **Olive oil**: 1 teaspoon
- **Vegetable broth**: 1¼ cups
- **Salt and black pepper**: To taste
- **Optional garnish**: Fresh parsley

Instructions

1. **Cook the Sausage**: Heat **olive oil** in a pot. Cook **sausage** slices until browned. Remove and set aside.
2. **Sauté Aromatics**: In the same pot, sauté **onion** and **garlic** for 2–3 minutes.
3. **Simmer the Stew**: Add **potatoes**, **kale**, and **vegetable broth**. Simmer for 20 minutes until the potatoes are tender.
4. **Combine and Serve**: Return the **sausage** to the pot and heat through. Season with **salt** and **pepper**. Garnish with parsley.

Tips and Tricks

- For added depth, use smoked sausage.
- Add a pinch of red pepper flakes for a hint of spice.

White Bean and Kale Soup

Serves: 1 | Prep Time: 10 mins | Cook Time: 25 mins

Ingredients

- **Kale**: 1 cup (chopped, stems removed)
- **White beans**: ¼ cup (cooked)
- **Carrot**: ¼ cup (sliced)
- **Onion**: ¼ medium (chopped)
- **Garlic**: 1 clove (minced)
- **Olive oil**: 1 teaspoon
- **Vegetable broth**: 1¼ cups
- **Thyme**: ¼ teaspoon (dried or fresh)
- **Salt and black pepper**: To taste
- **Optional garnish**: Grated Parmesan

Instructions

1. **Sauté Aromatics**: Heat **olive oil** in a pot. Sauté **onion**, **garlic**, and **thyme** for 2–3 minutes.
2. **Add Beans and Carrots**: Stir in **white beans** and **carrot** and cook for 3 minutes.
3. **Simmer the Soup**: Add **kale** and **vegetable broth**, simmering for 15–20 minutes.
4. **Season and Serve**: Adjust seasoning with **salt** and **pepper**. Garnish with grated Parmesan.

Tips and Tricks

- For a creamier texture, partially blend the soup.
- Add a squeeze of lemon juice to brighten the flavors.

Spicy Kale and Lentil Chili

Serves: 1 | Prep Time: 10 mins | Cook Time: 30 mins

Ingredients

- **Kale**: 1 cup (chopped, stems removed)
- **Red lentils**: ¼ cup (rinsed)
- **Tomato**: ½ medium (chopped)
- **Onion**: ¼ medium (chopped)
- **Garlic**: 1 clove (minced)
- **Chili powder**: ½ teaspoon
- **Cumin**: ½ teaspoon
- **Vegetable broth**: 1¼ cups
- **Olive oil**: 1 teaspoon
- **Salt and black pepper**: To taste
- **Optional garnish**: Sour cream

Instructions

1. **Sauté Aromatics**: Heat **olive oil** in a pot. Add **onion**, **garlic**, **chili powder**, and **cumin**, cooking for 2–3 minutes.
2. **Add Lentils and Tomato**: Stir in **lentils** and **tomato**. Cook for 2 minutes.
3. **Simmer the Chili**: Add **kale** and **vegetable broth**. Simmer for 20 minutes until the lentils are tender.
4. **Season and Serve**: Adjust seasoning with **salt** and **pepper**. Garnish with sour cream.

Tips and Tricks

- Add diced bell peppers for extra flavor.
- For added richness, stir in a dollop of yogurt or coconut cream.

Kale and Sweet Potato Soup

Serves: 1 | Prep Time: 10 mins | Cook Time: 25 mins

Ingredients

- **Kale**: 1 cup (chopped, stems removed)
- **Sweet potato**: ½ cup (cubed)
- **Onion**: ¼ medium (chopped)
- **Garlic**: 1 clove (minced)
- **Vegetable broth**: 1¼ cups
- **Ground cinnamon**: ¼ teaspoon
- **Olive oil**: 1 teaspoon
- **Salt and black pepper**: To taste
- **Optional garnish**: Crushed walnuts

Instructions

1. **Sauté Aromatics**: Heat **olive oil** in a pot. Add **onion**, **garlic**, and **cinnamon**, cooking for 2–3 minutes.
2. **Cook Vegetables**: Add **sweet potato** and cook for 5 minutes.
3. **Simmer the Soup**: Add **kale** and **vegetable broth**, simmering for 15–20 minutes until the sweet potato is tender.
4. **Blend and Serve**: Blend the soup partially for a creamy texture or leave chunky. Season with **salt** and **pepper**. Garnish with crushed walnuts.

Tips and Tricks

- Roast the sweet potato beforehand for a deeper flavor.
- Add a sprinkle of nutmeg for a warm, aromatic touch.

Benefits of Kale Soups

Benefit	Why It's Great
Winter Superfood	Kale thrives in winter and is packed with nutrients like vitamins A, C, and K.
Boosts Immunity	High in vitamin C, it helps strengthen your immune system during cold months.
Rich in Antioxidants	Helps fight inflammation and supports overall health in the winter chill.
Supports Bone Health	Contains calcium and vitamin K, important for maintaining strong bones.
Keeps You Full	The fiber in kale makes soups hearty and satisfying, perfect for colder weather.
Seasonally Fresh	Kale is a winter crop, so it's fresh, flavorful, and easy to find in the season.
Low-Calorie Powerhouse	Offers a nutrient-dense, low-calorie option for healthy eating.
Hydration in Dry Weather	Soups keep you hydrated, and kale adds a refreshing, earthy flavor.
Versatile and Delicious	Works well with winter flavors like garlic, onions, and smoked paprika.
Mood Booster	A bowl of kale soup provides warmth and comfort, fighting off winter blues.

Tip: Add crispy kale chips or a drizzle of olive oil as a garnish for an extra crunch and flavor boost!

Beans

Smoky Black Bean Chili

Serves: 1 | Prep Time: 10 mins | Cook Time: 30 mins

Ingredients

- **Black beans**: ½ cup (cooked)
- **Tomato**: ½ medium (chopped)
- **Onion**: ¼ medium (chopped)
- **Garlic**: 1 clove (minced)
- **Chili powder**: ½ teaspoon
- **Smoked paprika**: ½ teaspoon
- **Cumin**: ½ teaspoon
- **Vegetable broth**: 1¼ cups
- **Olive oil**: 1 teaspoon
- **Salt and black pepper**: To taste
- **Optional garnish**: Sour cream and chopped cilantro

Instructions

1. **Sauté Aromatics**: Heat **olive oil** in a pot. Add **onion**, **garlic**, **chili powder**, **paprika**, and **cumin**, cooking for 3 minutes.
2. **Add Beans and Tomato**: Stir in **black beans** and **tomato**, cooking for 2–3 minutes.
3. **Simmer the Chili**: Add **vegetable broth** and simmer for 20 minutes.
4. **Season and Serve**: Adjust seasoning with **salt** and **pepper**. Garnish with sour cream and chopped cilantro.

Tips and Tricks

- Add a splash of lime juice for brightness.
- For extra depth, stir in a teaspoon of dark cocoa powder.

Three-Bean Stew

Serves: 1 | Prep Time: 10 mins | Cook Time: 30 mins

Ingredients

- **Black beans**: ¼ cup (cooked)
- **Kidney beans**: ¼ cup (cooked)
- **Chickpeas**: ¼ cup (cooked)
- **Carrot**: ¼ cup (sliced)
- **Onion**: ¼ medium (chopped)
- **Garlic**: 1 clove (minced)
- **Thyme**: ¼ teaspoon (dried or fresh)
- **Vegetable broth**: 1¼ cups
- **Olive oil**: 1 teaspoon
- **Salt and black pepper**: To taste
- **Optional garnish**: Chopped parsley

Instructions

1. **Sauté Aromatics**: Heat **olive oil** in a pot. Add **onion**, **garlic**, and **thyme**, and cook for 3 minutes.
2. **Add Beans and Carrot**: Stir in **black beans**, **kidney beans**, **chickpeas**, and **carrot**. Cook for 3 minutes.
3. **Simmer the Stew**: Add **vegetable broth** and simmer for 20–25 minutes.
4. **Season and Serve**: Adjust seasoning with **salt** and **pepper**. Garnish with chopped parsley.

Tips and Tricks

- Add a dash of balsamic vinegar for a tangy kick.
- Serve with crusty bread for a heartier meal.

White Bean and Rosemary Soup

Serves: 1 | Prep Time: 10 mins | Cook Time: 25 mins

Ingredients

- **White beans**: ½ cup (cooked)
- **Onion**: ¼ medium (chopped)
- **Garlic**: 1 clove (minced)
- **Rosemary**: ¼ teaspoon (chopped, fresh or dried)
- **Vegetable broth**: 1¼ cups
- **Olive oil**: 1 teaspoon
- **Salt and black pepper**: To taste
- **Optional garnish**: Fresh rosemary sprig

Instructions

1. **Sauté Aromatics**: Heat **olive oil** in a pot. Add **onion**, **garlic**, and **rosemary**, and cook for 3 minutes.
2. **Add Beans and Simmer**: Stir in **white beans** and **vegetable broth**. Simmer for 15–20 minutes.
3. **Blend and Serve**: Blend the soup partially for a creamy texture while leaving some beans whole. Season with **salt** and **pepper**. Garnish with a rosemary sprig.

Tips and Tricks

- Add a drizzle of truffle oil for an indulgent touch.
- Serve with grated Parmesan for extra richness.

Green Bean and Bacon Soup

Serves: 1 | Prep Time: 10 mins | Cook Time: 25 mins

Ingredients

- **Green beans**: ½ cup (chopped)
- **Bacon**: 1 slice (chopped)
- **Potato**: ¼ cup (diced)
- **Onion**: ¼ medium (chopped)
- **Garlic**: 1 clove (minced)
- **Vegetable broth**: 1¼ cups
- **Salt and black pepper**: To taste
- **Optional garnish**: Crumbled bacon

Instructions

1. **Cook the Bacon**: In a pot, cook **bacon** until crispy. Remove and set aside.
2. **Sauté Vegetables**: In the bacon drippings, sauté **onion**, **garlic**, and **potato** for 3–4 minutes.
3. **Simmer the Soup**: Add **green beans** and **vegetable broth**, simmering for 15–20 minutes.
4. **Season and Serve**: Adjust seasoning with **salt** and **pepper**. Garnish with crumbled bacon.

Tips and Tricks

- For a smoky flavor, use smoked bacon.
- Stir in a splash of cream for a silky texture.

Benefits of Bean Soups

Benefit	Why It's Great
Rich in Protein	Beans provide plant-based protein, keeping you full and energized in the cold.
Packed with Fiber	Supports digestion and keeps you satisfied for longer on chilly days.
Budget-Friendly	Affordable and easy to store, beans are perfect for cost-effective winter meals.
Immune Boosting	High in antioxidants and vitamins, beans help your body fight off winter illnesses.
Warm and Comforting	Bean soups are hearty, warming, and perfect for cozy evenings.
Nutrient-Dense	Beans are full of iron, magnesium, and potassium, which are essential for health.
Energy Sustainer	Complex carbs in beans provide long-lasting energy during colder months.
Versatile for Flavors	Beans pair beautifully with winter herbs and spices like rosemary, thyme, and cumin.
Supports Heart Health	Low in fat and high in fiber, beans help maintain a healthy heart.
Hydration with Texture	Soups hydrate while beans add a satisfying bite, perfect for dry winter air.

Tip: Garnish with a swirl of olive oil, fresh herbs, or a sprinkle of smoked paprika for extra flavor!

Barley

Beef and Barley Stew

Serves: 1 | Prep Time: 15 mins | Cook Time: 40 mins

Ingredients

- **Beef chunks**: ¼ cup
- **Barley**: ¼ cup
- **Carrot**: ¼ cup (sliced)
- **Celery**: ¼ cup (chopped)
- **Onion**: ¼ medium (chopped)
- **Garlic**: 1 clove (minced)
- **Vegetable or beef broth**: 1½ cups
- **Olive oil**: 1 teaspoon
- **Thyme**: ¼ teaspoon (dried or fresh)
- **Salt and black pepper**: To taste
- **Optional garnish**: Fresh parsley

Instructions

1. **Sear the Beef**: Heat **olive oil** in a pot. Brown the **beef chunks** for 3–4 minutes, then remove and set aside.
2. **Sauté Aromatics**: In the same pot, sauté **onion**, **garlic**, **carrot**, and **celery** for 3–4 minutes.
3. **Combine and Simmer**: Add the seared **beef**, **barley**, **broth**, and **thyme**. Simmer for 30 minutes until the barley is tender.
4. **Season and Serve**: Adjust seasoning with **salt** and **pepper**. Garnish with fresh parsley.

Tips and Tricks

- For added depth, deglaze the pot with a splash of red wine before adding the broth.
- Use bone broth for richer flavor and nutrition.

Mushroom and Barley Soup

Serves: 1 | Prep Time: 10 mins | Cook Time: 30 mins

Ingredients

- **Barley**: ¼ cup
- **Mushrooms**: ½ cup (sliced)
- **Onion**: ¼ medium (chopped)
- **Garlic**: 1 clove (minced)
- **Vegetable broth**: 1½ cups
- **Olive oil**: 1 teaspoon
- **Thyme**: ¼ teaspoon (dried or fresh)
- **Salt and black pepper**: To taste
- **Optional garnish**: Chopped parsley

Instructions

1. **Sauté Aromatics**: Heat **olive oil** in a pot. Add **onion**, **garlic**, and **thyme**, cooking for 2–3 minutes.
2. **Cook Mushrooms**: Stir in **mushrooms** and cook for 5 minutes until softened.
3. **Simmer with Barley**: Add **barley** and **vegetable broth**. Simmer for 20–25 minutes until the barley is tender.
4. **Season and Serve**: Adjust seasoning with **salt** and **pepper**. Garnish with chopped parsley.

Tips and Tricks

- For a smoky touch, add a pinch of smoked paprika.
- Use a mix of wild mushrooms for enhanced flavor.

Barley and Winter Vegetable Chowder

Serves: 1 | Prep Time: 15 mins | Cook Time: 30 mins

Ingredients

- **Barley**: ¼ cup
- **Parsnip**: ¼ cup (diced)
- **Turnip**: ¼ cup (diced)
- **Carrot**: ¼ cup (sliced)
- **Onion**: ¼ medium (chopped)
- **Vegetable broth**: 1½ cups
- **Whole milk or cream**: ¼ cup
- **Olive oil**: 1 teaspoon
- **Salt and black pepper**: To taste
- **Optional garnish**: Fresh thyme sprig

Instructions

1. **Sauté Vegetables**: Heat **olive oil** in a pot. Sauté **onion**, **parsnip**, **turnip**, and **carrot** for 5 minutes.
2. **Simmer with Barley**: Add **barley** and **vegetable broth**, simmering for 20 minutes until tender.
3. **Stir in Cream**: Stir in **milk or cream** and heat gently. Do not boil.
4. **Season and Serve**: Adjust seasoning with **salt** and **pepper**. Garnish with a thyme sprig.

Tips and Tricks

- Add a pinch of nutmeg for a warming aroma.
- For added texture, roast the vegetables before simmering.

Tomato Barley and Spinach Soup

Serves: 1 | Prep Time: 10 mins | Cook Time: 25 mins

Ingredients

- **Barley**: ¼ cup
- **Tomatoes**: ½ cup (chopped)
- **Spinach**: 1 cup (chopped)
- **Garlic**: 1 clove (minced)
- **Onion**: ¼ medium (chopped)
- **Vegetable broth**: 1½ cups
- **Olive oil**: 1 teaspoon
- **Italian seasoning**: ¼ teaspoon
- **Salt and black pepper**: To taste
- **Optional garnish**: Grated Parmesan

Instructions

1. **Sauté Aromatics**: Heat **olive oil** in a pot. Add **onion**, **garlic**, and **Italian seasoning**, cooking for 2–3 minutes.
2. **Add Tomatoes and Barley**: Stir in **tomatoes** and **barley**, cooking for 3 minutes.
3. **Simmer the Soup**: Add **vegetable broth** and simmer for 20 minutes until the barley is tender.
4. **Stir in Spinach**: Add **spinach** during the last 5 minutes of cooking.
5. **Season and Serve**: Adjust seasoning with **salt** and **pepper**. Garnish with grated Parmesan.

Tips and Tricks

- For a richer taste, add a splash of balsamic vinegar.
- Use fire-roasted tomatoes for enhanced flavor.

Benefits of Barley Soups

Benefit	Why It's Great
Hearty and Filling	Barley's chewy texture and complex carbs make soups satisfying and perfect for winter.
Rich in Fiber	Supports digestion and keeps you full on cold days, reducing cravings for snacks.
Provides Warmth	A bowl of barley soup warms you up and provides comfort in chilly weather.
Boosts Energy	Barley's slow-releasing carbohydrates offer sustained energy during shorter days.
Supports Heart Health	Contains beta-glucans, which help lower cholesterol and improve heart health.
Affordable and Accessible	Barley is budget-friendly and easy to store, making it ideal for winter cooking.
Immune Support	High in nutrients like zinc and selenium, barley helps boost your immune system.
Hydration with Bulk	Soups hydrate you while barley adds bulk for a more substantial meal.
Versatile with Flavors	Works well with winter vegetables like carrots, celery, and turnips, and spices like thyme or bay leaves.
Supports Bone Health	Barley contains minerals like magnesium and phosphorus, essential for strong bones.

Tip: Garnish with a sprinkle of fresh parsley or a drizzle of lemon juice to brighten the flavors!

Beef and Ham

Classic Beef and Vegetable Stew

Serves: 1 | Prep Time: 15 mins | Cook Time: 40 mins

Ingredients

- **Beef chunks**: ¼ cup
- **Potato**: ½ cup (diced)
- **Carrot**: ¼ cup (sliced)
- **Celery**: ¼ cup (chopped)
- **Onion**: ¼ medium (chopped)
- **Garlic**: 1 clove (minced)
- **Vegetable or beef broth**: 1½ cups
- **Tomato paste**: 1 teaspoon
- **Olive oil**: 1 teaspoon
- **Thyme**: ¼ teaspoon (dried or fresh)
- **Salt and black pepper**: To taste

Instructions

1. **Sear the Beef**: Heat **olive oil** in a pot. Brown the **beef chunks** for 3–4 minutes, then remove and set aside.
2. **Sauté Vegetables**: In the same pot, sauté **onion**, **garlic**, **carrot**, and **celery** for 5 minutes.
3. **Simmer the Stew**: Add **potatoes**, **broth**, **tomato paste**, and **thyme**. Return the beef and simmer for 30 minutes until tender.
4. **Season and Serve**: Adjust seasoning with **salt** and **pepper**.

Tips and Tricks

- Add a splash of red wine for depth of flavor.
- Stir in frozen peas in the last 5 minutes for a touch of sweetness.

Smoky Split Pea and Ham Soup

Serves: 1 | Prep Time: 10 mins | Cook Time: 30 mins

Ingredients

- **Split peas**: ¼ cup (rinsed)
- **Ham**: ¼ cup (diced)
- **Carrot**: ¼ cup (diced)
- **Celery**: ¼ cup (chopped)
- **Onion**: ¼ medium (chopped)
- **Garlic**: 1 clove (minced)
- **Vegetable or ham broth**: 1½ cups
- **Smoked paprika**: ¼ teaspoon
- **Olive oil**: 1 teaspoon
- **Salt and black pepper**: To taste
- **Optional garnish**: Croutons

Instructions

1. **Sauté Vegetables**: Heat **olive oil** in a pot. Add **onion**, **garlic**, **carrot**, and **celery**, and cook for 5 minutes.
2. **Add Peas and Ham**: Stir in **split peas**, **ham**, and **smoked paprika**. Cook for 2 minutes.
3. **Simmer the Soup**: Add **broth** and simmer for 25 minutes until peas are soft.
4. **Season and Serve**: Adjust seasoning with **salt** and **pepper**. Garnish with croutons if desired.

Tips and Tricks

- For a creamier texture, blend half the soup.
- Add a bay leaf while simmering for a subtle herbal note.

Ground Beef and Lentil Chili

Serves: 1 | Prep Time: 10 mins | Cook Time: 30 mins

Ingredients

- **Ground beef**: ¼ cup
- **Red lentils**: ¼ cup (rinsed)
- **Tomato**: ½ medium (chopped)
- **Onion**: ¼ medium (chopped)
- **Garlic**: 1 clove (minced)
- **Chili powder**: ½ teaspoon
- **Cumin**: ½ teaspoon
- **Vegetable broth**: 1½ cups
- **Olive oil**: 1 teaspoon
- **Salt and black pepper**: To taste
- **Optional garnish**: Sour cream

Instructions

1. **Brown the Beef**: Heat **olive oil** in a pot. Add **ground beef** and cook until browned, breaking it into small pieces. Remove excess fat if necessary.
2. **Sauté Aromatics**: Stir in **onion**, **garlic**, **chili powder**, and **cumin**, cooking for 3 minutes.
3. **Simmer the Chili**: Add **lentils**, **tomato**, and **broth**. Simmer for 20 minutes until lentils are tender.
4. **Season and Serve**: Adjust seasoning with **salt** and **pepper**. Garnish with sour cream.

Tips and Tricks

- Add a splash of apple cider vinegar for tanginess.
- Use fire-roasted tomatoes for added depth.

Braised Ham and Bean Stew

Serves: 1 | Prep Time: 10 mins | Cook Time: 35 mins

Ingredients

- **Ham**: ¼ cup (diced)
- **White beans**: ¼ cup (cooked)
- **Carrot**: ¼ cup (sliced)
- **Celery**: ¼ cup (chopped)
- **Onion**: ¼ medium (chopped)
- **Garlic**: 1 clove (minced)
- **Vegetable or ham broth**: 1½ cups
- **Thyme**: ¼ teaspoon (dried or fresh)
- **Olive oil**: 1 teaspoon
- **Salt and black pepper**: To taste

Instructions

1. **Sauté Ham and Vegetables**: Heat **olive oil** in a pot. Sauté **ham**, **onion**, **garlic**, **carrot**, and **celery** for 5 minutes.
2. **Simmer with Beans**: Add **white beans**, **broth**, and **thyme**. Simmer for 25 minutes.
3. **Season and Serve**: Adjust seasoning with **salt** and **pepper**.

Tips and Tricks

- Add a pinch of red pepper flakes for heat.
- Serve with cornbread for a classic pairing.

Benefits of Beef and Ham Soups

Benefit	Why It's Great
Rich in Protein	Both beef and ham provide high-quality protein, essential for muscle repair and energy.
Hearty and Satisfying	Perfect for cold winter days, these meats make soups filling and comforting.
Energy Boost	Beef and ham are rich in iron, which helps combat winter fatigue by supporting red blood cells.
Immune Support	Zinc in beef boosts your immune system to fight off winter colds and flu.
Source of Minerals	Beef and ham provide important nutrients like phosphorus, selenium, and B vitamins.
Keeps You Warm	Hearty meat soups provide the calories and warmth your body craves during winter.
Versatile Flavor Profiles	Combine with beans, potatoes, or winter greens like kale for nutrient-rich soups.
Supports Bone Health	If using beef bones for broth, soups are rich in collagen, which is good for joints and skin.
Customizable Heaviness	Adjust richness with cream or balance with vegetables for a lighter option.
Mood-Boosting Comfort	Warm, savory beef and ham soups uplift spirits on cold, gloomy days.

Tip: Garnish with crispy fried onions or a dollop of sour cream for added texture and flavor!

Clams

New England Clam Chowder

Serves: 1 | Prep Time: 10 mins | Cook Time: 25 mins

Ingredients

- **Clams**: ¼ cup (chopped, cooked, or canned)
- **Potato**: ½ cup (diced)
- **Onion**: ¼ medium (chopped)
- **Celery**: ¼ cup (chopped)
- **Garlic**: 1 clove (minced)
- **Whole milk or cream**: ½ cup
- **Vegetable broth**: 1 cup
- **Butter**: 1 teaspoon
- **Flour**: ½ teaspoon (optional, for thickening)
- **Salt and black pepper**: To taste
- **Optional garnish**: Chopped parsley or oyster crackers

Instructions

1. **Sauté Aromatics**: Heat **butter** in a pot. Add **onion**, **garlic**, and **celery**, cooking for 3 minutes.
2. **Cook Potatoes**: Add **potato** and sauté for 2 minutes.
3. **Simmer the Soup**: Stir in **broth** and cook for 15 minutes until the potato is tender.
4. **Add Clams and Milk**: Stir in **clams** and **milk**. Heat gently, but do not boil. Adjust consistency with **flour** if needed.
5. **Season and Serve**: Season with **salt** and **pepper**. Garnish with parsley or oyster crackers.

Tips and Tricks

- Use fresh clams for the best flavor—steam and chop before adding to the soup.
- Add a dash of white wine for extra depth.

Creamy Clam and Corn Soup

Serves: 1 | Prep Time: 10 mins | Cook Time: 20 mins

Ingredients

- **Clams**: ¼ cup (chopped, cooked, or canned)
- **Sweet corn**: ½ cup (kernels)
- **Potato**: ¼ cup (diced)
- **Onion**: ¼ medium (chopped)
- **Vegetable broth**: 1 cup
- **Whole milk or cream**: ½ cup
- **Butter**: 1 teaspoon
- **Paprika**: ¼ teaspoon
- **Salt and black pepper**: To taste
- **Optional garnish**: Crumbled bacon or chopped parsley

Instructions

1. **Sauté Aromatics**: Heat **butter** in a pot. Add **onion** and sauté for 3 minutes.
2. **Simmer Vegetables**: Add **potato**, **corn**, and **broth**, cooking for 15 minutes until the potato is tender.
3. **Add Clams and Milk**: Stir in **clams**, **milk**, and **paprika**. Heat gently, but do not boil.
4. **Season and Serve**: Season with **salt** and **pepper**. Garnish with crumbled bacon or parsley.

Tips and Tricks

- Use smoked paprika for added depth.
- Stir in a splash of clam juice for an extra boost of flavor.

Bacon and Clam Stew

Serves: 1 | Prep Time: 10 mins | Cook Time: 30 mins

Ingredients

- **Clams**: ¼ cup (chopped, cooked, or canned)
- **Bacon**: 1 slice (chopped)
- **Potato**: ¼ cup (diced)
- **Onion**: ¼ medium (chopped)
- **Celery**: ¼ cup (chopped)
- **Vegetable broth**: 1 cup
- **Whole milk or cream**: ¼ cup
- **Thyme**: ¼ teaspoon (dried or fresh)
- **Salt and black pepper**: To taste
- **Optional garnish**: Crumbled bacon

Instructions

1. **Cook the Bacon**: In a pot, cook **bacon** until crispy. Remove and set aside.
2. **Sauté Vegetables**: In the bacon drippings, sauté **onion**, **celery**, and **potato** for 5 minutes.
3. **Simmer the Stew**: Add **broth** and simmer for 15 minutes until the potato is tender.
4. **Add Clams and Milk**: Stir in **clams**, **milk**, and **thyme**. Heat gently without boiling.
5. **Season and Serve**: Adjust seasoning and garnish with crumbled bacon.

Tips and Tricks

- Add a splash of sherry for a richer stew.
- Pair with crusty bread for a hearty meal.

Manhattan Clam Chowder

Serves: 1 | Prep Time: 10 mins | Cook Time: 25 mins

Ingredients

- **Clams**: ¼ cup (chopped, cooked, or canned)
- **Tomato**: ½ medium (chopped)
- **Potato**: ¼ cup (diced)
- **Carrot**: ¼ cup (sliced)
- **Celery**: ¼ cup (chopped)
- **Onion**: ¼ medium (chopped)
- **Garlic**: 1 clove (minced)
- **Vegetable broth**: 1½ cups
- **Olive oil**: 1 teaspoon
- **Thyme**: ¼ teaspoon (dried or fresh)
- **Salt and black pepper**: To taste
- **Optional garnish**: Fresh parsley

Instructions

1. **Sauté Aromatics**: Heat **olive oil** in a pot. Add **onion**, **garlic**, **carrot**, and **celery**, and cook for 5 minutes.
2. **Add Potatoes and Tomatoes**: Stir in **potato**, **tomato**, and **broth**. Simmer for 15 minutes.
3. **Add Clams and Thyme**: Stir in **clams** and **thyme**, cooking for 5 more minutes.
4. **Season and Serve**: Adjust seasoning with **salt** and **pepper**. Garnish with parsley.

Tips and Tricks

- Use diced fire-roasted tomatoes for a smokier flavor.
- Add a dash of hot sauce for a spicy kick.

Benefits of Clam Soups

Benefit	Why It's Great
Rich in Protein	Clams are a lean source of protein, keeping you full and energized in the cold.
Immune Boosting	High in zinc, clams help strengthen your immune system during flu season.
Source of Iron	Clams provide a significant amount of iron, which combats winter fatigue and anemia.
Supports Heart Health	Rich in omega-3 fatty acids, clams contribute to a healthy heart and circulation.
Warm and Comforting	A creamy clam chowder is perfect for cozying up on a cold winter day.
Low-Calorie Option	When prepared without heavy cream, clam soups are light yet satisfying.
Rich in Minerals	Clams are packed with selenium, magnesium, and phosphorus, supporting overall health.
Hydration and Nourishment	Soups provide hydration, while clams add a flavorful, nutrient-dense component.
Pairs with Winter Staples	Works beautifully with potatoes, leeks, and celery for a hearty winter soup.
Comfort Food Appeal	The savory, oceanic flavor of clams creates a luxurious and mood-boosting experience.

Tip: Add fresh herbs like parsley and a squeeze of lemon for a bright and refreshing finish to your clam soup!

Celery Root

Creamy Celery Root and Potato Soup

Serves: 1 | Prep Time: 10 mins | Cook Time: 25 mins

Ingredients

- **Celery root**: ½ cup (peeled and diced)
- **Potato**: ½ cup (diced)
- **Onion**: ¼ medium (chopped)
- **Garlic**: 1 clove (minced)
- **Vegetable broth**: 1½ cups
- **Whole milk or cream**: ¼ cup
- **Olive oil**: 1 teaspoon
- **Salt and black pepper**: To taste
- **Optional garnish**: Chopped chives

Instructions

1. **Sauté Aromatics**: Heat **olive oil** in a pot. Add **onion** and **garlic**, cooking for 3 minutes.
2. **Cook Vegetables**: Add **celery root** and **potato**, stirring well. Cook for 5 minutes.
3. **Simmer the Soup**: Add **vegetable broth** and simmer for 15–20 minutes until vegetables are tender.
4. **Blend and Add Milk**: Blend the soup until smooth. Stir in **milk or cream**, heating gently.
5. **Season and Serve**: Season with **salt** and **pepper**. Garnish with chopped chives.

Tips and Tricks

- Add a pinch of nutmeg for a warm, earthy flavor.
- Roast the celery root beforehand for a deeper, caramelized taste.

Celery Root and Apple Bisque

Serves: 1 | Prep Time: 10 mins | Cook Time: 25 mins

Ingredients

- **Celery root**: ½ cup (peeled and diced)
- **Apple**: ½ medium (peeled and chopped)
- **Onion**: ¼ medium (chopped)
- **Vegetable broth**: 1½ cups
- **Whole milk or cream**: ¼ cup
- **Butter**: 1 teaspoon
- **Ground nutmeg**: ¼ teaspoon
- **Salt and black pepper**: To taste
- **Optional garnish**: Apple slices or a drizzle of olive oil

Instructions

1. **Sauté Aromatics**: Heat **butter** in a pot. Add **onion** and cook for 3 minutes.
2. **Add Celery Root and Apple**: Stir in **celery root** and **apple**, cooking for 5 minutes.
3. **Simmer the Bisque**: Add **vegetable broth** and simmer for 15–20 minutes until the celery root is tender.
4. **Blend and Add Milk**: Blend the soup until smooth. Stir in **milk or cream**.
5. **Season and Serve**: Season with **salt**, **pepper**, and **nutmeg**. Garnish with apple slices.

Tips and Tricks

- For a touch of sweetness, drizzle honey over the bisque before serving.
- Use tart apples like Granny Smith for a balanced flavor.

Celery Root and Carrot Soup

Serves: 1 | Prep Time: 10 mins | Cook Time: 25 mins

Ingredients

- **Celery root**: ½ cup (peeled and diced)
- **Carrot**: ½ cup (sliced)
- **Onion**: ¼ medium (chopped)
- **Garlic**: 1 clove (minced)
- **Vegetable broth**: 1½ cups
- **Olive oil**: 1 teaspoon
- **Ground cumin**: ¼ teaspoon
- **Salt and black pepper**: To taste
- **Optional garnish**: Fresh parsley

Instructions

1. **Sauté Aromatics**: Heat **olive oil** in a pot. Add **onion**, **garlic**, and **cumin**, cooking for 3 minutes.
2. **Cook Vegetables**: Add **celery root** and **carrot**, stirring well. Cook for 5 minutes.

3. **Simmer the Soup**: Add **vegetable broth** and simmer for 15–20 minutes until the vegetables are tender.
4. **Blend and Serve**: Blend the soup until smooth. Adjust seasoning with **salt** and **pepper**. Garnish with parsley.

Tips and Tricks

- Add a pinch of smoked paprika for a hint of depth.
- Pair with crusty bread for a satisfying meal.

Roasted Celery Root and Leek Soup

Serves: 1 | Prep Time: 15 mins | Cook Time: 30 mins

Ingredients

- **Celery root**: ½ cup (peeled and cubed)
- **Leek**: ½ medium (sliced, white and light green parts only)
- **Garlic**: 1 clove (whole)
- **Vegetable broth**: 1½ cups
- **Olive oil**: 1 teaspoon
- **Salt and black pepper**: To taste
- **Optional garnish**: Croutons or fresh thyme

Instructions

1. **Roast the Vegetables**: Preheat oven to 400°F (200°C). Toss **celery root** and **garlic** with **olive oil**, season with **salt** and **pepper**, and roast for 20 minutes until golden.
2. **Cook the Leek**: Heat **olive oil** in a pot. Add **leek** and sauté for 5 minutes.
3. **Simmer the Soup**: Add the roasted **celery root** and **garlic** to the pot with **vegetable broth**. Simmer for 10 minutes.
4. **Blend and Serve**: Blend the soup until smooth. Adjust seasoning with **salt** and **pepper**. Garnish with croutons or thyme.

Tips and Tricks

- Roast a sprig of thyme alongside the vegetables for extra flavor.
- Add a splash of white wine before simmering for a refined touch.

Benefits of Celery Root Soups

Benefit	Why It's Great
Warmth and Comfort	A creamy celery root soup is cozy and perfect for cold winter days.
Rich in Nutrients	Packed with vitamins C and K, celery root supports your immune system and bone health.
Low-Calorie Option	Celery root is naturally low in calories, making soups healthy and guilt-free.
Rich in Fiber	High fiber content aids digestion and keeps you feeling full longer.
Hydration in Winter	Soups with celery root provide both hydration and nourishment during the dry season.
Heart-Healthy	Contains potassium, which helps regulate blood pressure and supports heart health.
Versatile Flavor	Mild and nutty, celery root pairs well with winter herbs like thyme and bay leaves.
Boosts Energy	A good source of complex carbs, it provides a steady energy boost in cold weather.
Budget-Friendly	Affordable and long-lasting, celery root is a great choice for winter cooking.
Light and Refreshing	Its earthy flavor and creamy texture balance heavier winter meals.

Tip: Garnish with a drizzle of truffle oil, fresh parsley, or toasted seeds for extra flavor and texture!

Kabocha Squash

Roasted Kabocha Squash and Ginger Soup

Serves: 1 | Prep Time: 15 mins | Cook Time: 30 mins

Ingredients

- **Kabocha squash**: 1 cup (peeled and cubed)
- **Ginger**: ½ teaspoon (grated)
- **Onion**: ¼ medium (chopped)
- **Garlic**: 1 clove (whole)
- **Vegetable broth**: 1½ cups
- **Olive oil**: 1 teaspoon
- **Salt and black pepper**: To taste
- **Optional garnish**: Fresh cilantro or roasted pumpkin seeds

Instructions

1. **Roast the Squash**: Preheat oven to 400°F (200°C). Toss **kabocha squash** and **garlic** with **olive oil**, and roast for 20 minutes until caramelized.
2. **Sauté Aromatics**: Heat **olive oil** in a pot. Add **onion** and **ginger**, cooking for 3 minutes.
3. **Simmer the Soup**: Add roasted **kabocha squash**, **garlic**, and **vegetable broth**. Simmer for 10 minutes.
4. **Blend and Season**: Blend the soup until smooth. Adjust seasoning with **salt** and **pepper**. Garnish with cilantro or pumpkin seeds.

Tips and Tricks

- For extra flavor, drizzle the squash with a bit of honey before roasting.
- Add a splash of coconut milk for added creaminess.

Creamy Kabocha and Coconut Soup

Serves: 1 | Prep Time: 10 mins | Cook Time: 25 mins

Ingredients

- **Kabocha squash**: 1 cup (peeled and cubed)
- **Coconut milk**: ½ cup
- **Vegetable broth**: 1½ cups
- **Ginger**: ½ teaspoon (grated)
- **Garlic**: 1 clove (minced)
- **Olive oil**: 1 teaspoon
- **Ground turmeric**: ¼ teaspoon
- **Salt and black pepper**: To taste
- **Optional garnish**: Fresh cilantro

Instructions

1. **Sauté Aromatics**: Heat **olive oil** in a pot. Add **garlic**, **ginger**, and **turmeric**, and cook for 2 minutes.
2. **Cook Squash**: Stir in **kabocha squash** and sauté for 5 minutes.
3. **Simmer the Soup**: Add **coconut milk** and **vegetable broth**, simmering for 15 minutes until the squash is tender.
4. **Blend and Serve**: Blend the soup until smooth. Adjust seasoning with **salt** and **pepper**. Garnish with cilantro.

Tips and Tricks

- Add a pinch of chili flakes for a spicy kick.
- Serve with a side of naan or crusty bread for a complete meal.

Kabocha Squash and Lentil Stew

Serves: 1 | Prep Time: 10 mins | Cook Time: 30 mins

Ingredients

- **Kabocha squash**: 1 cup (peeled and cubed)
- **Red lentils**: ¼ cup (rinsed)
- **Carrot**: ¼ cup (sliced)
- **Onion**: ¼ medium (chopped)
- **Garlic**: 1 clove (minced)
- **Vegetable broth**: 1½ cups
- **Ground cumin**: ½ teaspoon
- **Olive oil**: 1 teaspoon
- **Salt and black pepper**: To taste
- **Optional garnish**: Chopped parsley

Instructions

1. **Sauté Aromatics**: Heat **olive oil** in a pot. Add **onion**, **garlic**, and **cumin**, cooking for 3 minutes.
2. **Add Vegetables and Lentils**: Stir in **kabocha squash**, **carrot**, and **lentils**, cooking for 2 minutes.
3. **Simmer the Stew**: Add **vegetable broth** and simmer for 25 minutes until the lentils and squash are tender.
4. **Season and Serve**: Adjust seasoning with **salt** and **pepper**. Garnish with parsley.

Tips and Tricks

- Add a splash of lemon juice to brighten the flavors.
- Sprinkle toasted nuts for added texture and crunch.

Spiced Kabocha Squash Chowder

Serves: 1 | Prep Time: 10 mins | Cook Time: 30 mins

Ingredients

- **Kabocha squash**: 1 cup (peeled and cubed)
- **Potato**: ½ cup (diced)
- **Onion**: ¼ medium (chopped)
- **Garlic**: 1 clove (minced)
- **Vegetable broth**: 1½ cups
- **Whole milk or cream**: ¼ cup
- **Ground cinnamon**: ¼ teaspoon
- **Ground nutmeg**: ¼ teaspoon
- **Olive oil**: 1 teaspoon
- **Salt and black pepper**: To taste
- **Optional garnish**: Croutons

Instructions

1. **Sauté Aromatics**: Heat **olive oil** in a pot. Add **onion**, **garlic**, **cinnamon**, and **nutmeg**, cooking for 3 minutes.
2. **Cook Vegetables**: Add **kabocha squash** and **potato**, cooking for 5 minutes.
3. **Simmer the Chowder**: Add **vegetable broth** and simmer for 20 minutes until the squash is tender.
4. **Blend and Add Milk**: Blend the soup partially for a creamy texture. Stir in **milk or cream** and heat gently.
5. **Season and Serve**: Adjust seasoning with **salt** and **pepper**. Garnish with croutons.

Tips and Tricks

- Add a pinch of cayenne for a spicy edge.
- Use roasted kabocha squash for deeper flavor.

Benefits of Kabocha Squash Soups

Benefit	Why It's Great
Warm and Comforting	A bowl of creamy kabocha squash soup provides cozy warmth on cold winter days.
Rich in Vitamin A	High in beta-carotene, kabocha supports eye health and boosts the immune system.
Low-Calorie and Filling	Naturally low in calories yet creamy and satisfying, perfect for light winter meals.
Packed with Fiber	Supports digestion and keeps you feeling full and nourished during chilly weather.
Supports Heart Health	Contains potassium and antioxidants that help regulate blood pressure and protect the heart.
Seasonal Freshness	Kabocha squash is at its peak in winter, ensuring a flavorful and nutritious soup.
Boosts Immunity	High in vitamin C, kabocha helps ward off colds and flu common in winter months.
Versatile and Flavorful	Pairs well with spices like ginger, nutmeg, and cinnamon for a sweet-savory balance.
Energy Boost	Complex carbs provide steady energy, keeping you active even on sluggish winter days.
Mood-Boosting Comfort	Its natural sweetness and creamy texture uplift the spirit during dark, cold days.

Tip: Garnish with roasted kabocha seeds, a swirl of coconut cream, or a sprinkle of toasted nuts for extra crunch and flavor!

Spring: Fresh and Vibrant
Asparagus

Creamy Asparagus and Potato Soup for One

Serves: 1 | Prep Time: 10 mins | Cook Time: 20 mins

Ingredients

- **Fresh asparagus**: 4 spears
- **Potato**: 1 small
- **Onion**: ¼ medium, chopped
- **Vegetable broth**: 1 cup
- **Whole milk or cream**: ¼ cup
- **Olive oil**: 1 teaspoon
- **Garlic**: ½ clove
- **Fresh thyme**: ¼ teaspoon
- **Salt**: To taste
- **Black pepper**: To taste
- **Optional garnish**: Parmesan or croutons

Instructions

1. **Prepare the Base**: Heat **olive oil** in a small pot over medium heat. Add the **chopped onion** and **minced garlic**. Sauté until softened, about 2–3 minutes. Stir in **thyme** and cook for another 30 seconds.
2. **Cook the Vegetables**: Add the **diced potato** and **asparagus**. Stir well to coat. Pour in the **vegetable broth** and bring to a boil. Lower to a simmer and cook for 15 minutes or until tender.
3. **Blend for Creaminess**: Remove from heat. Puree the soup with an immersion blender or in a standard blender, then return to the pot.
4. **Finish with Cream**: Stir in the **milk or cream**. Heat gently over low heat without boiling. Season with **salt** and **pepper**.
5. **Serve and Enjoy**: Garnish with **Parmesan**, **croutons**, or a drizzle of **olive oil**, if desired.

Lemon Asparagus Soup for One

Serves: 1 | Prep Time: 10 mins | Cook Time: 20 mins

Ingredients

- **Fresh asparagus**: 4 spears
- **Vegetable broth**: 1 cup
- **Lemon zest**: ½ teaspoon
- **Lemon juice**: 1 teaspoon
- **Shallot**: 1 small, chopped
- **Olive oil**: 1 teaspoon
- **Garlic**: ½ clove
- **Salt**: To taste
- **Black pepper**: To taste
- **Fresh dill (optional)**: ¼ teaspoon
- **Optional garnish**: Lemon slice

Instructions

1. **Sauté the Shallot**: Heat **olive oil** in a small pot over medium heat. Add the **chopped shallot** and **minced garlic**. Cook for 2–3 minutes until softened.
2. **Add the Asparagus**: Add **chopped asparagus** to the pot and cook for another 2 minutes, stirring frequently.
3. **Simmer with Broth**: Pour in the **vegetable broth** and bring to a boil. Reduce heat and simmer for 15 minutes until the asparagus is tender.
4. **Blend and Add Lemon**: Blend the soup until smooth using an immersion blender. Stir in **lemon zest** and **juice**. Season with **salt** and **pepper**.
5. **Serve and Garnish**: Pour into a bowl and garnish with a **lemon slice** or a sprinkle of **fresh dill**, if desired.

Asparagus and Spring Herb Chowder for One

Serves: 1 | Prep Time: 10 mins | Cook Time: 25 mins

Ingredients

- **Fresh asparagus**: 4 spears
- **Potato**: 1 small
- **Vegetable broth**: 1 cup
- **Whole milk or cream**: ¼ cup
- **Onion**: ¼ medium, chopped
- **Garlic**: ½ clove
- **Fresh parsley**: ½ teaspoon
- **Fresh chives**: ½ teaspoon
- **Olive oil**: 1 teaspoon
- **Salt**: To taste
- **Black pepper**: To taste
- **Optional garnish**: Fresh herbs

Instructions

1. **Prepare the Base**: Heat **olive oil** in a small pot over medium heat. Add the **onion** and **garlic**. Sauté for 3–4 minutes until fragrant.
2. **Add Vegetables and Broth**: Add the **potato, asparagus**, and **broth**. Bring to a boil, then reduce to a simmer for 15 minutes.
3. **Blend Partially**: Remove half of the soup and puree it until smooth. Return the blended portion to the pot, creating a creamy yet chunky texture.
4. **Finish with Milk and Herbs**: Stir in the **milk or cream, parsley**, and **chives**. Heat gently and season with **salt** and **pepper**.
5. **Serve and Garnish**: Garnish with extra **herbs** and enjoy warm.

Roasted Asparagus and Garlic Soup for One

Serves: 1 | Prep Time: 10 mins | Cook Time: 30 mins

Ingredients

- **Fresh asparagus**: 4 spears
- **Garlic**: 1 clove
- **Vegetable broth**: 1 cup
- **Olive oil**: 1 teaspoon
- **Onion**: ¼ medium, chopped
- **Salt**: To taste
- **Black pepper**: To taste
- **Lemon juice**: ½ teaspoon
- **Optional garnish**: Croutons or basil

Instructions

1. **Roast the Asparagus and Garlic**: Preheat oven to 400°F (200°C). Toss **asparagus** and **garlic** with **olive oil, salt**, and **pepper**. Roast on a baking sheet for 15 minutes.
2. **Sauté Aromatics**: In a small pot, sauté **onion** in **olive oil** over medium heat until softened (2–3 minutes).
3. **Combine and Simmer**: Add roasted **asparagus, garlic**, and **vegetable broth**. Bring to a boil, then simmer for 10 minutes.
4. **Blend and Season**: Puree the soup until smooth. Stir in **lemon juice** and adjust seasoning with **salt** and **pepper**.
5. **Serve and Garnish**: Top with **croutons** or fresh **basil** and serve hot.

Benefits of Asparagus Soups

Benefit	Why It's Great
Rich in Vitamins	Asparagus is packed with vitamins A, C, E, and K, which support your immune system and overall health.
Detoxifying	High in antioxidants, asparagus helps flush out toxins, making it a great spring detox food.
Supports Digestion	Rich in fiber and prebiotics, asparagus promotes healthy digestion and gut health.
Boosts Energy	Asparagus provides a natural energy boost, perfect for longer, sunnier spring days.
Low-Calorie and Light	Asparagus is low in calories but high in nutrients, making it a perfect light spring meal.
Hydration	Asparagus is made up of over 90% water, helping you stay hydrated during warmer weather.
Mood-Lifting	The natural folate in asparagus helps improve mood and may reduce stress and anxiety.
Supports Heart Health	Asparagus contains potassium and antioxidants that help regulate blood pressure and support cardiovascular health.
Seasonal Freshness	Fresh asparagus is abundant in spring, offering the best flavor and nutrients during this season.
Customizable Flavor	Pairs beautifully with fresh herbs like dill, parsley, and lemon for a bright, spring-inspired flavor.

Tip: Add a dollop of crème fraîche or a sprinkle of lemon zest to brighten the flavors and add extra creaminess to your asparagus soup!

Peas

Spring Pea and Mint Soup for One

Serves: 1 | Prep Time: 10 mins | Cook Time: 15 mins

Ingredients

- **Fresh peas**: 1 cup
- **Vegetable broth**: 1 cup
- **Fresh mint leaves**: 4 large, chopped
- **Olive oil**: 1 teaspoon
- **Onion**: ¼ medium, chopped
- **Garlic**: ½ clove
- **Lemon juice**: ½ teaspoon
- **Salt**: To taste
- **Black pepper**: To taste

Instructions

1. **Sauté Aromatics**: Heat **olive oil** in a small pot over medium heat. Add the **onion** and **garlic**. Cook for 2–3 minutes until softened.
2. **Cook the Peas**: Add the **peas** and **vegetable broth**. Bring to a boil, then reduce heat to a simmer. Cook for 5–7 minutes until the peas are tender.
3. **Blend with Mint**: Remove from heat and blend the soup with an immersion blender or in a standard blender until smooth. Stir in **lemon juice** and **mint leaves**.
4. **Season and Serve**: Adjust seasoning with **salt** and **pepper**. Garnish with a dollop of **sour cream**, if desired.

Pea and Parmesan Broth for One

Serves: 1 | Prep Time: 5 mins | Cook Time: 15 mins

Ingredients

- **Fresh peas**: ¾ cup
- **Vegetable broth**: 1 cup
- **Parmesan rind**: 1 small piece
- **Garlic**: ½ clove
- **Olive oil**: 1 teaspoon
- **Salt**: To taste
- **Black pepper**: To taste
- **Optional garnish**: Grated Parmesan

Instructions

1. **Prepare the Base**: Heat **olive oil** in a small pot. Add the **garlic** and cook for 1–2 minutes until fragrant.
2. **Simmer with Parmesan**: Add the **vegetable broth**, **peas**, and **Parmesan rind**. Bring to a boil, then simmer gently for 10 minutes to infuse the broth.
3. **Remove the Rind**: Discard the **Parmesan rind** and lightly mash the peas with the back of a spoon for a rustic texture.
4. **Season and Serve**: Adjust seasoning with **salt** and **pepper**. Garnish with freshly grated **Parmesan**, if desired.

Pea and Ham Stew for One

Serves: 1 | Prep Time: 10 mins | Cook Time: 25 mins

Ingredients

- **Fresh peas**: 1 cup
- **Ham (diced)**: ¼ cup
- **Potato**: 1 small, diced
- **Vegetable broth**: 1 cup
- **Onion**: ¼ medium, chopped
- **Olive oil**: 1 teaspoon
- **Garlic**: ½ clove
- **Fresh parsley**: ½ teaspoon
- **Salt**: To taste
- **Black pepper**: To taste

Instructions

1. **Sauté Aromatics**: Heat **olive oil** in a pot. Add the **onion** and **garlic**, sautéing until softened (2–3 minutes).
2. **Cook the Ham and Vegetables**: Add the **ham**, **potato**, and **peas** to the pot. Stir for 2 minutes.
3. **Simmer**: Pour in the **vegetable broth** and bring to a boil. Lower to a simmer and cook for 15–20 minutes, or until the potato is tender.
4. **Season and Garnish**: Adjust seasoning with **salt** and **pepper**. Garnish with chopped **parsley** or **croutons**, if desired.

Chilled Pea and Tarragon Soup for One

Serves: 1 | Prep Time: 10 mins | Cook Time: 10 mins + Chill Time

Ingredients

- **Fresh peas**: 1 cup
- **Vegetable broth**: ½ cup
- **Whole milk or cream**: ¼ cup
- **Garlic**: ½ clove
- **Fresh tarragon**: ½ teaspoon
- **Olive oil**: 1 teaspoon
- **Lemon juice**: ½ teaspoon
- **Salt**: To taste
- **Black pepper**: To taste

Instructions

1. **Cook the Peas**: Heat **olive oil** in a small pot. Add the **garlic** and sauté until fragrant (1–2 minutes). Add **peas** and **vegetable broth**, simmering for 5–7 minutes.
2. **Blend Smooth**: Remove from heat and blend the soup until smooth. Stir in **milk or cream**, **lemon juice**, and **tarragon**.
3. **Chill**: Transfer the soup to a container and refrigerate for at least 1 hour.
4. **Serve and Enjoy**: Pour into a bowl, adjust seasoning with **salt** and **pepper**, and serve cold.

Benefits of Pea Soups

Benefit	Why It's Great
Rich in Protein	Peas are a great plant-based protein source, helping to build and repair tissues.
Packed with Fiber	High in fiber, peas support digestion and keep you feeling full and satisfied.
Immune Support	Full of vitamin C, peas help boost the immune system, keeping you healthy in spring.
Low-Calorie and Light	Pea soup is light yet filling, making it perfect for spring when you crave something fresh but hearty.
Rich in Antioxidants	Peas are rich in antioxidants that fight free radicals and reduce inflammation.
Supports Heart Health	High in potassium, peas help maintain healthy blood pressure and support heart function.
Boosts Energy	The combination of carbohydrates and protein provides steady energy for active spring days.
Hydration	Peas have a high water content, helping keep you hydrated during warmer spring weather.
Seasonal Freshness	Fresh peas in spring offer the best flavor and nutrition, making them ideal for soups.
Mood-Boosting	The folate content in peas may improve mood and reduce feelings of stress or fatigue.

Spinach and Leeks

Spinach and Leek Soup with Lemon Zest for One

Serves: 1 | Prep Time: 10 mins | Cook Time: 20 mins

Ingredients

- **Spinach (fresh)**: 1 cup
- **Leek (sliced)**: ½ medium
- **Vegetable broth**: 1 cup
- **Olive oil**: 1 teaspoon
- **Garlic**: ½ clove
- **Lemon zest**: ½ teaspoon
- **Lemon juice**: ½ teaspoon
- **Salt**: To taste
- **Black pepper**: To taste
- **Optional garnish**: Croutons or cream

Instructions

1. **Sauté the Leek**: Heat **olive oil** in a small pot over medium heat. Add the sliced **leek** and cook for 3–4 minutes until softened.
2. **Add Garlic and Spinach**: Stir in the **garlic** and cook for 1 minute. Add the **spinach** and cook until wilted, about 2 minutes.
3. **Simmer the Soup**: Pour in the **vegetable broth**, bring to a boil, then reduce to a simmer. Cook for 10 minutes.
4. **Blend and Finish**: Remove the soup from heat and blend until smooth. Stir in **lemon zest** and **juice**, and season with **salt** and **pepper**.
5. **Serve and Garnish**: Pour into a bowl and garnish with **croutons** or a swirl of cream, if desired.

Creamy Spinach and Garlic Soup for One

Serves: 1 | Prep Time: 10 mins | Cook Time: 15 mins

Ingredients

- **Spinach (fresh)**: 1½ cups
- **Garlic**: 1 clove
- **Vegetable broth**: 1 cup
- **Whole milk or cream**: ¼ cup
- **Olive oil**: 1 teaspoon
- **Salt**: To taste
- **Black pepper**: To taste
- **Optional garnish**: Parmesan

Instructions

1. **Sauté the Garlic**: Heat **olive oil** in a small pot over medium heat. Add the minced **garlic** and cook for 1–2 minutes until fragrant.
2. **Cook the Spinach**: Add the **spinach** to the pot and sauté until wilted, about 2 minutes.
3. **Simmer the Soup**: Pour in the **vegetable broth** and bring to a boil. Reduce heat and simmer for 5 minutes.
4. **Blend and Add Cream**: Blend the soup until smooth. Stir in the **milk or cream** and season with **salt** and **pepper**.
5. **Serve and Garnish**: Garnish with grated **Parmesan** or a drizzle of olive oil, if desired.

Tips and Tricks

- **Make It More Flavorful:** Add a pinch of nutmeg or lemon zest to enhance the soup's flavor, creating a more complex and aromatic taste.
- **Add a Protein Boost:** For extra protein, stir in some cooked chicken or beans when blending the soup. This makes it more filling without compromising the creamy texture.

Leek and Barley Stew for One

Serves: 1 | Prep Time: 15 mins | Cook Time: 40 mins

Ingredients

- **Leek (sliced)**: 1 medium
- **Pearl barley**: ¼ cup
- **Vegetable broth**: 1¼ cups
- **Carrot (diced)**: ¼ medium
- **Celery (diced)**: 1 stalk
- **Olive oil**: 1 teaspoon
- **Garlic**: ½ clove
- **Fresh thyme**: ¼ teaspoon
- **Salt**: To taste
- **Black pepper**: To taste
- **Optional garnish**: Fresh parsley

Instructions

1. **Sauté Aromatics**: Heat **olive oil** in a small pot over medium heat. Add the sliced **leek**, **carrot**, and **celery**, cooking for 5 minutes.
2. **Add Barley and Broth**: Stir in the **garlic**, **thyme**, and **barley**. Pour in the **vegetable broth** and bring to a boil.
3. **Simmer**: Reduce heat to low and simmer for 30 minutes, or until the barley is tender. Stir occasionally to prevent sticking.
4. **Season and Garnish**: Adjust seasoning with **salt** and **pepper**. Serve hot, garnished with fresh **parsley**, if desired.

Tips and Tricks

- **Make it Heartier:** Add cooked beans or chicken to the stew for an extra boost of protein, making it a more filling meal.
- **Creamy Twist:** Stir in a splash of coconut milk or heavy cream at the end for a creamy, rich texture.

Spinach and White Bean Soup for One

Serves: 1 | Prep Time: 10 mins | Cook Time: 20 mins

Ingredients

- **Spinach (fresh)**: 1 cup
- **White beans (canned)**: ½ cup
- **Vegetable broth**: 1 cup
- **Onion (chopped)**: ¼ medium
- **Garlic**: ½ clove
- **Olive oil**: 1 teaspoon
- **Lemon juice**: ½ teaspoon
- **Salt**: To taste
- **Black pepper**: To taste

Instructions

1. **Sauté the Onion and Garlic**: Heat **olive oil** in a small pot. Add **onion** and **garlic** and cook for 2–3 minutes until softened.
2. **Add Beans and Broth**: Stir in the **white beans** and **vegetable broth**. Bring to a boil, then reduce to a simmer for 10 minutes.
3. **Add Spinach**: Stir in the **spinach** and cook until wilted, about 2–3 minutes.
4. **Season and Finish**: Stir in **lemon juice** and season with **salt** and **pepper**. Serve hot.

Benefits of Spinach and Leek Soups

Benefit	Why It's Great
Rich in Nutrients	Spinach is high in vitamins A, C, and K, while leeks provide a mild, onion-like flavor packed with antioxidants.
Boosts Immune System	Both spinach and leeks are rich in vitamin C, helping to strengthen your immune system during the spring season.
Supports Digestion	Leeks contain prebiotics that promote healthy gut bacteria, while spinach adds fiber for smooth digestion.
Low-Calorie and Light	Spinach and leeks are naturally low in calories, making this soup a great option for light spring meals.
Boosts Energy	Packed with iron and folate, spinach helps combat fatigue and keeps you energized throughout the day.
Heart Health	Leeks are rich in flavonoids that support heart health by reducing cholesterol and improving circulation.
Mood-Boosting	The folate and magnesium in spinach may help lift your mood and reduce stress or anxiety.
Detoxifying	Spinach helps detoxify the body and reduce inflammation, a great springtime cleanse for your system.

Carrots and Herbs

Carrot and Ginger Soup

Serves: 1 | Prep Time: 10 mins | Cook Time: 20 mins

Ingredients

- **Carrots (chopped)**: 1 cup
- **Ginger (grated)**: ½ teaspoon
- **Vegetable broth**: 1 cup
- **Onion (chopped)**: ¼ medium
- **Garlic**: ½ clove
- **Olive oil**: 1 teaspoon
- **Lemon juice**: ½ teaspoon
- **Salt**: To taste
- **Black pepper**: To taste
- **Optional garnish**: Yogurt swirl or parsley

Instructions

1. **Sauté Aromatics**: Heat **olive oil** in a small pot over medium heat. Add **onion**, **garlic**, and **ginger**. Sauté for 3 minutes until fragrant.
2. **Add Carrots and Broth**: Add the **carrots** and pour in the **vegetable broth**. Bring to a boil, then reduce to a simmer. Cook for 15 minutes or until the carrots are tender.
3. **Blend and Season**: Remove from heat and blend the soup until smooth. Stir in **lemon juice** and season with **salt** and **pepper**.
4. **Serve and Garnish**: Garnish with a swirl of yogurt or fresh parsley, if desired.

Creamy Carrot and Dill Chowder

Serves: 1 | Prep Time: 10 mins | Cook Time: 25 mins

Ingredients

- **Carrots (chopped)**: 1 cup
- **Potato (diced)**: 1 small
- **Vegetable broth**: 1 cup
- **Whole milk or cream**: ¼ cup
- **Garlic**: ½ clove
- **Dill (chopped)**: ½ teaspoon
- **Onion (chopped)**: ¼ medium
- **Olive oil**: 1 teaspoon
- **Salt**: To taste
- **Black pepper**: To taste
- **Optional garnish**: Dill sprigs

Instructions

1. **Sauté Aromatics**: Heat **olive oil** in a small pot over medium heat. Add the **onion** and **garlic**. Cook for 2–3 minutes until softened.
2. **Cook the Vegetables**: Add the **carrots**, **potato**, and **vegetable broth**. Bring to a boil, then reduce to a simmer. Cook for 15–20 minutes until the vegetables are tender.
3. **Blend and Add Cream**: Blend the soup until smooth. Stir in the **milk or cream** and **dill**. Heat gently but do not boil.
4. **Season and Serve**: Adjust seasoning with **salt** and **pepper**. Garnish with fresh **dill sprigs** and serve.

Tips and Tricks

- **Enhance the Flavor:** Add a splash of lemon juice or zest at the end to brighten the flavors and balance the richness of the cream.
- **Make It Chunkier:** For a heartier texture, blend only half of the soup and leave the rest of the vegetables in chunks for a more rustic chowder.

Carrot, Lentil, and Thyme Stew

Serves: 1 | Prep Time: 15 mins | Cook Time: 30 mins

Ingredients

- **Carrots (chopped)**: ¾ cup
- **Red lentils (rinsed)**: ¼ cup
- **Vegetable broth**: 1 cup
- **Onion (chopped)**: ¼ medium
- **Garlic**: ½ clove
- **Olive oil**: 1 teaspoon
- **Fresh thyme**: ¼ teaspoon
- **Lemon juice**: ½ teaspoon
- **Salt**: To taste
- **Black pepper**: To taste
- **Optional garnish**: Crusty bread

Instructions

1. **Sauté Aromatics**: Heat **olive oil** in a small pot. Add the **onion**, **garlic**, and **thyme**, and sauté for 3 minutes.
2. **Add Carrots and Lentils**: Stir in the **carrots** and **lentils**, cooking for 1–2 minutes.
3. **Simmer**: Add the **vegetable broth**, bring to a boil, then reduce to a simmer. Cook for 20–25 minutes until the lentils and carrots are tender.
4. **Season and Serve**: Stir in **lemon juice** and adjust seasoning with **salt** and **pepper**. Serve with crusty bread.

Herb-Roasted Carrot and Parsnip Soup

Serves: 1 | Prep Time: 10 mins | Cook Time: 30 mins

Ingredients

- **Carrots (chopped)**: ½ cup
- **Parsnips (chopped)**: ½ cup
- **Vegetable broth**: 1 cup
- **Olive oil**: 1 teaspoon
- **Garlic**: ½ clove
- **Fresh parsley**: ½ teaspoon
- **Salt**: To taste
- **Black pepper**: To taste
- **Optional garnish**: Croutons

Instructions

1. **Roast the Vegetables**: Preheat oven to 400°F (200°C). Toss **carrots** and **parsnips** with **olive oil**, **salt**, and **pepper**. Roast on a baking sheet for 20 minutes or until tender.
2. **Sauté the Garlic**: Heat a small pot over medium heat and sauté **garlic** for 1 minute.
3. **Simmer and Blend**: Add the roasted **carrots** and **parsnips** to the pot. Pour in **vegetable broth**, simmer for 5 minutes, then blend until smooth.
4. **Season and Serve**: Adjust seasoning with **salt** and **pepper**. Garnish with fresh **parsley** or croutons.

Benefits of Carrot and Herb Soups

Benefit	Why It's Great
Rich in Vitamin A	Carrots are high in beta-carotene, which supports eye health and boosts your immune system.
Boosts Immune System	The combination of carrots and fresh herbs like parsley and thyme provides a vitamin-packed boost to your immunity.
Hydration	Carrots have a high water content, helping you stay hydrated as the temperatures warm up in spring.
Rich in Antioxidants	Carrots and herbs are full of antioxidants that help fight inflammation and support overall health.
Supports Digestion	High in fiber, carrots promote healthy digestion, while herbs like parsley can soothe the digestive system.
Low-Calorie and Light	A low-calorie, light soup, perfect for spring when you crave fresh and healthy meals.
Supports Skin Health	The vitamin A in carrots supports skin health, promoting a healthy glow as the weather changes.
Detoxifying	Herbs like parsley aid in detoxifying the body, making it a great spring cleanse.
Energizing	Carrots provide natural sugars that give you a quick energy boost, ideal for the active spring season.
Mood-Boosting	Fresh herbs can have a calming effect, while carrots' nutrients can help reduce stress and boost mood.

Tip: Add a touch of ginger or lemon to enhance the fresh, bright flavors and add extra zing to your carrot and herb soup!

Artichokes

Artichoke and Fennel Soup

Serves: 1 | Prep Time: 10 mins | Cook Time: 30 mins

Ingredients

- **Artichoke hearts**: ½ cup
- **Fennel bulb (sliced)**: ¼ medium
- **Vegetable broth**: 1 cup
- **Onion (chopped)**: ¼ medium
- **Garlic**: ½ clove
- **Olive oil**: 1 teaspoon
- **Lemon juice**: ½ teaspoon
- **Salt**: To taste
- **Black pepper**: To taste
- **Optional garnish**: Fennel fronds

Instructions

1. **Sauté Aromatics**: Heat **olive oil** in a small pot over medium heat. Add **onion**, **garlic**, and **fennel slices**. Cook for 5–7 minutes until softened.
2. **Add Artichokes and Broth**: Stir in the **artichoke hearts** and pour in the **vegetable broth**. Bring to a boil, then lower to a simmer. Cook for 20 minutes until all vegetables are tender.
3. **Blend and Season**: Blend the soup until smooth. Stir in **lemon juice** and season with **salt** and **pepper**.
4. **Serve and Garnish**: Pour into a bowl and garnish with fresh **fennel fronds**.

Creamy Artichoke and Lemon Soup

Serves: 1 | Prep Time: 10 mins | Cook Time: 25 mins

Ingredients

- **Artichoke hearts**: ½ cup
- **Vegetable broth**: 1 cup
- **Whole milk or cream**: ¼ cup
- **Garlic**: ½ clove
- **Onion (chopped)**: ¼ medium
- **Lemon zest**: ½ teaspoon
- **Lemon juice**: ½ teaspoon
- **Olive oil**: 1 teaspoon
- **Salt**: To taste
- **Black pepper**: To taste
- **Optional garnish**: Lemon slice

Instructions

1. **Sauté Aromatics**: Heat **olive oil** in a small pot. Add **onion** and **garlic** and cook for 3 minutes until fragrant.
2. **Add Artichokes and Broth**: Stir in the **artichoke hearts** and **vegetable broth**. Simmer for 15 minutes until tender.
3. **Blend and Add Cream**: Blend the soup until smooth. Stir in the **milk or cream**, **lemon zest**, and **juice**. Heat gently, but avoid boiling.
4. **Season and Serve**: Adjust seasoning with **salt** and **pepper**. Garnish with a **lemon slice**, if desired.

Artichoke and Spring Vegetable Stew

Serves: 1 | Prep Time: 15 mins | Cook Time: 30 mins

Ingredients

- **Artichoke hearts**: ½ cup
- **Asparagus (chopped)**: ¼ cup
- **Peas (fresh)**: ¼ cup
- **Vegetable broth**: 1¼ cups
- **Potato (diced)**: 1 small
- **Olive oil**: 1 teaspoon
- **Garlic**: ½ clove
- **Fresh parsley**: ½ teaspoon
- **Salt**: To taste
- **Black pepper**: To taste
- **Optional garnish**: Fresh parsley

Instructions

1. **Sauté Aromatics**: Heat **olive oil** in a pot over medium heat. Add **garlic** and sauté for 1 minute until fragrant.
2. **Cook Vegetables**: Add **artichoke hearts**, **asparagus**, and **potatoes**. Stir and cook for 5 minutes.
3. **Simmer**: Pour in the **vegetable broth**, bring to a boil, then reduce to a simmer. Cook for 20 minutes until the potatoes are tender. Add the **peas** during the last 5 minutes of cooking.
4. **Season and Serve**: Adjust seasoning with **salt** and **pepper**. Garnish with fresh **parsley** and serve warm.

Tips and Tricks

- **Add More Herbs:** Enhance the flavor with additional fresh herbs like thyme or rosemary. You can add them during the simmering stage for more depth.
- **Make It Heartier:** For a richer texture, blend half of the soup and return it to the pot, giving the stew a creamy consistency without adding cream.

Braised Artichoke and Potato Soup

Serves: 1 | Prep Time: 15 mins | Cook Time: 35 mins

Ingredients

- **Artichoke hearts**: ½ cup
- **Potato (diced)**: 1 small
- **Vegetable broth**: 1¼ cups
- **Onion (chopped)**: ¼ medium
- **Garlic**: ½ clove
- **Olive oil**: 1 teaspoon
- **Fresh thyme**: ¼ teaspoon
- **Lemon juice**: ½ teaspoon
- **Salt**: To taste
- **Black pepper**: To taste
- **Optional garnish**: Croutons

Instructions

1. **Sauté Aromatics**: Heat **olive oil** in a pot. Add **onion** and **garlic**, cooking for 3 minutes.
2. **Braise Artichokes**: Add **artichoke hearts** and cook for 5 minutes, stirring occasionally.
3. **Simmer with Potatoes**: Add the **potatoes**, **vegetable broth**, and **thyme**. Bring to a boil, then reduce to a simmer. Cook for 25 minutes until tender.
4. **Season and Serve**: Stir in **lemon juice** and adjust seasoning with **salt** and **pepper**. Garnish with croutons, if desired.

Benefits of Artichoke Soups

Benefit	Why It's Great
Rich in Antioxidants	Artichokes are high in antioxidants like cynarin, which help fight inflammation and support liver health.
Supports Digestive Health	Artichokes are known for improving digestion by promoting healthy bile production, making them great for a spring cleanse.
Low-Calorie and Nutritious	Artichokes are low in calories but rich in vitamins and minerals, offering a nutrient-dense option for light spring meals.
Promotes Heart Health	Rich in fiber and potassium, artichokes help regulate cholesterol levels and support heart health.
Detoxifying	Artichokes aid in detoxification, promoting healthy liver function and the elimination of toxins.
Rich in Fiber	High in fiber, artichokes support digestion and keep you feeling full, making them a satisfying yet light spring meal.

Spring Onions

Spring Onion and Potato Soup

Serves: 1 | Prep Time: 10 mins | Cook Time: 25 mins

Ingredients

- **Spring onions (sliced)**: 3 medium
- **Potato (diced)**: 1 small
- **Vegetable broth**: 1 cup
- **Olive oil**: 1 teaspoon
- **Garlic**: ½ clove
- **Salt**: To taste
- **Black pepper**: To taste
- **Optional garnish**: Fresh parsley

Instructions

1. **Sauté Aromatics**: Heat **olive oil** in a small pot over medium heat. Add the **sliced spring onions** and **garlic**, and sauté for 2–3 minutes until softened.
2. **Add Potatoes and Broth**: Stir in the **potato** and pour in the **vegetable broth**. Bring to a boil, then reduce to a simmer. Cook for 20 minutes until the potatoes are tender.
3. **Blend and Season**: Remove from heat and blend the soup until smooth. Season with **salt** and **pepper**.
4. **Serve and Garnish**: Pour into a bowl and garnish with chopped **parsley**, if desired.

Spring Onion and Mushroom Broth

Serves: 1 | Prep Time: 10 mins | Cook Time: 20 mins

Ingredients

- **Spring onions (sliced)**: 2 medium
- **Mushrooms (sliced)**: ½ cup
- **Vegetable broth**: 1¼ cups
- **Garlic**: ½ clove
- **Soy sauce**: ½ teaspoon
- **Olive oil**: 1 teaspoon
- **Salt**: To taste
- **Black pepper**: To taste
- **Optional garnish**: Spring onion greens

Instructions

1. **Sauté Vegetables**: Heat **olive oil** in a small pot over medium heat. Add **spring onions** and **mushrooms**, and cook for 5 minutes until softened.
2. **Simmer the Broth**: Add the **vegetable broth**, **garlic**, and **soy sauce**. Bring to a boil, then simmer for 10 minutes.
3. **Season and Serve**: Adjust seasoning with **salt** and **pepper**. Garnish with sliced **spring onion greens** and serve hot.

Tips and Tricks

- **Add a Protein Boost:** For added protein, try stirring in tofu, tempeh, or even cooked chicken during the simmering stage.
- **Enhance the Umami:** Add a few drops of sesame oil or a small spoonful of miso paste to deepen the flavor of the broth and give it a richer umami taste.

Lemon and Spring Onion Soup

Serves: 1 | Prep Time: 10 mins | Cook Time: 20 mins

Ingredients

- **Spring onions (sliced)**: 3 medium
- **Vegetable broth**: 1 cup
- **Lemon zest**: ½ teaspoon
- **Lemon juice**: ½ teaspoon
- **Garlic**: ½ clove
- **Olive oil**: 1 teaspoon
- **Salt**: To taste
- **Black pepper**: To taste
- **Optional garnish**: Lemon slice

Instructions

1. **Sauté Aromatics**: Heat **olive oil** in a small pot over medium heat. Add the **spring onions** and **garlic**, and cook for 3 minutes.
2. **Simmer the Soup**: Add the **vegetable broth**, bring to a boil, then reduce to a simmer. Cook for 10 minutes.
3. **Add Lemon Flavor**: Stir in **lemon zest** and **juice**. Adjust seasoning with **salt** and **pepper**.
4. **Serve and Garnish**: Garnish with a slice of **lemon** and serve warm.

Creamy Spring Onion and Asparagus Soup

Serves: 1 | Prep Time: 10 mins | Cook Time: 25 mins

Ingredients

- **Spring onions (sliced)**: 2 medium
- **Asparagus (chopped)**: 4 spears
- **Vegetable broth**: 1 cup
- **Whole milk or cream**: ¼ cup
- **Garlic**: ½ clove
- **Olive oil**: 1 teaspoon
- **Salt**: To taste
- **Black pepper**: To taste
- **Optional garnish**: Asparagus tips

Instructions

1. **Sauté the Spring Onions**: Heat **olive oil** in a small pot over medium heat. Add the **spring onions** and **garlic**, and cook for 2–3 minutes.
2. **Add Asparagus and Broth**: Stir in the **asparagus** and **vegetable broth**. Bring to a boil, then simmer for 15 minutes until the asparagus is tender.
3. **Blend and Add Cream**: Blend the soup until smooth. Stir in the **milk or cream**. Heat gently, but do not boil.
4. **Season and Serve**: Adjust seasoning with **salt** and **pepper**. Garnish with roasted **asparagus tips** if desired.

Benefits of Spring Onion Soups

Benefit	Why It's Great
Rich in Vitamins	Packed with vitamins A, C, and K, boosting immunity and skin health.
Supports Digestion	Contains prebiotics that promote healthy gut bacteria and digestion.
Low-Calorie & Light	Low in calories, making it perfect for light spring meals.
Anti-Inflammatory	Spring onions contain compounds that reduce inflammation.
Hydration	High water content helps you stay hydrated as the weather warms.
Supports Heart Health	Rich in antioxidants and potassium, promoting heart health and circulation.
Rich in Antioxidants	Helps fight free radicals and reduce oxidative stress.
Improves Skin Health	Vitamin C in spring onions supports collagen production for healthy skin.
Boosts Energy	Provides a mild natural energy boost, perfect for active spring days.

Tip: Garnish with fresh herbs or a squeeze of lemon to enhance the bright, fresh flavor!

Radishes

Chilled Radish and Dill Soup

Serves: 1 | Prep Time: 10 mins | Cook Time: 10 mins + Chill Time

Ingredients

- **Radishes (sliced)**: ½ cup
- **Vegetable broth**: ½ cup
- **Whole milk or cream**: ¼ cup
- **Garlic**: ½ clove
- **Fresh dill (chopped)**: ½ teaspoon
- **Lemon juice**: ½ teaspoon
- **Salt**: To taste
- **Black pepper**: To taste
- **Optional garnish**: Fresh dill sprigs

Instructions

1. **Cook the Radishes**: Heat a small pot and sauté **radishes** and **garlic** for 2–3 minutes. Add the **vegetable broth** and simmer for 5 minutes.
2. **Blend Smooth**: Remove from heat and blend until smooth. Stir in the **milk or cream**, **dill**, and **lemon juice**.
3. **Chill**: Refrigerate for at least 1 hour.
4. **Serve and Garnish**: Pour into a bowl and garnish with fresh **dill sprigs**. Serve cold.

Radish and Mint Broth

Serves: 1 | Prep Time: 5 mins | Cook Time: 15 mins

Ingredients

- **Radishes (sliced)**: ½ cup
- **Vegetable broth**: 1 cup
- **Fresh mint leaves**: ½ teaspoon
- **Garlic**: ½ clove
- **Olive oil**: 1 teaspoon
- **Salt**: To taste
- **Black pepper**: To taste
- **Optional garnish**: Mint sprig

Instructions

1. **Sauté the Radishes**: Heat **olive oil** in a small pot over medium heat. Add the **radishes** and sauté for 3 minutes.
2. **Simmer the Broth**: Pour in the **vegetable broth** and add the **garlic**. Simmer for 10 minutes.
3. **Add Mint and Season**: Stir in the **mint leaves** and cook for 1 additional minute. Adjust seasoning with **salt** and **pepper**.
4. **Serve and Garnish**: Pour into a bowl and garnish with a fresh **mint sprig**.

Radish and Spinach Soup

Serves: 1 | Prep Time: 10 mins | Cook Time: 15 mins

Ingredients

- **Radishes (sliced)**: ½ cup
- **Spinach (fresh)**: 1 cup
- **Vegetable broth**: 1 cup
- **Garlic**: ½ clove
- **Olive oil**: 1 teaspoon
- **Salt**: To taste
- **Black pepper**: To taste
- **Optional garnish**: Croutons

Instructions

1. **Sauté Aromatics**: Heat **olive oil** in a small pot over medium heat. Add the **radishes** and **garlic**, cooking for 3–4 minutes.
2. **Simmer the Soup**: Add the **spinach** and **vegetable broth**. Bring to a boil, then reduce heat and simmer for 10 minutes.
3. **Blend and Season**: Blend the soup until smooth. Adjust seasoning with **salt** and **pepper**.
4. **Serve and Garnish**: Garnish with croutons and serve warm.

Creamy Radish and Yogurt Soup

Serves: 1 | Prep Time: 10 mins | Cook Time: 10 mins

Ingredients

- **Radishes (sliced)**: ½ cup
- **Vegetable broth**: ½ cup
- **Plain yogurt**: ¼ cup
- **Garlic**: ½ clove
- **Olive oil**: 1 teaspoon
- **Fresh parsley**: ½ teaspoon
- **Salt**: To taste
- **Black pepper**: To taste
- **Optional garnish**: Radish slices

Instructions

1. **Sauté the Radishes**: Heat **olive oil** in a small pot over medium heat. Add the **radishes** and **garlic**, cooking for 2–3 minutes.
2. **Simmer and Blend**: Add the **vegetable broth** and cook for 5 minutes. Blend until smooth.
3. **Stir in Yogurt**: Remove from heat and stir in the **yogurt** and **parsley**. Adjust seasoning with **salt** and **pepper**.
4. **Serve and Garnish**: Garnish with sliced radishes and serve.

Benefits of Radish Soups

Benefit	Why It's Great
Rich in Vitamin C	Boosts immunity and supports skin health during spring.
Supports Digestion	High in fiber, radishes aid digestion and promote gut health.
Hydration	High water content helps you stay hydrated as temperatures rise.
Supports Skin Health	The antioxidants in radishes help maintain a healthy glow.
Rich in Fiber	Helps with digestion and keeps you full longer.
Boosts Circulation	Contains potassium, promoting healthy circulation and heart function.

Tip: Add a squeeze of lemon or fresh herbs for an extra refreshing kick!

Summer: Light and Refreshing
Tomatoes

Classic Gazpacho

Serves: 1 | Prep Time: 15 mins | No Cook Time

Ingredients

- **Tomatoes (ripe)**: 2 medium
- **Cucumber (peeled)**: ¼ medium
- **Red bell pepper**: ¼ medium
- **Garlic**: ½ clove
- **Olive oil**: 1 teaspoon
- **Red wine vinegar**: ½ teaspoon
- **Salt**: To taste
- **Black pepper**: To taste
- **Optional garnish**: Fresh basil

Instructions

1. **Prepare Vegetables**: Chop **tomatoes**, **cucumber**, and **bell pepper** into small pieces.
2. **Blend the Gazpacho**: In a blender, combine **tomatoes**, **cucumber**, **bell pepper**, **garlic**, **olive oil**, and **red wine vinegar**. Blend until smooth.
3. **Season and Chill**: Adjust seasoning with **salt** and **pepper**. Refrigerate for at least 1 hour.
4. **Serve and Garnish**: Pour into a bowl and garnish with fresh **basil** or extra diced vegetables.

Tomato and Basil Soup

Serves: 1 | Prep Time: 10 mins | Cook Time: 25 mins

Ingredients

- **Tomatoes (ripe)**: 2 medium
- **Vegetable broth**: 1 cup
- **Fresh basil leaves**: 4 large
- **Garlic**: ½ clove
- **Onion (chopped)**: ¼ medium
- **Olive oil**: 1 teaspoon
- **Salt**: To taste
- **Black pepper**: To taste
- **Optional garnish**: Basil sprig

Instructions

1. **Sauté Aromatics**: Heat **olive oil** in a small pot over medium heat. Add **onion** and **garlic**, cooking for 3 minutes until fragrant.
2. **Cook the Tomatoes**: Add the **chopped tomatoes** and cook for 5 minutes until softened.
3. **Simmer the Soup**: Pour in the **vegetable broth** and bring to a boil. Reduce heat and simmer for 15 minutes.
4. **Blend and Season**: Blend the soup until smooth. Stir in **basil leaves** and adjust seasoning with **salt** and **pepper**.
5. **Serve and Garnish**: Garnish with a sprig of fresh **basil** and serve warm.

Roasted Tomato and Red Pepper Soup

Serves: 1 | Prep Time: 10 mins | Cook Time: 30 mins

Ingredients

- **Tomatoes (halved)**: 2 medium
- **Red bell pepper**: ½ medium
- **Vegetable broth**: 1 cup
- **Garlic (whole)**: 1 clove
- **Olive oil**: 1 teaspoon
- **Salt**: To taste
- **Black pepper**: To taste
- **Optional garnish**: Basil leaves

Instructions

1. **Roast the Vegetables**: Preheat oven to 400°F (200°C). Place **tomatoes**, **red bell pepper**, and **garlic** on a baking sheet. Drizzle with **olive oil** and roast for 20 minutes.
2. **Simmer the Soup**: Transfer the roasted vegetables to a pot. Add the **vegetable broth** and simmer for 10 minutes.
3. **Blend and Season**: Blend the soup until smooth. Adjust seasoning with **salt** and **pepper**.
4. **Serve and Garnish**: Garnish with fresh **basil leaves** and serve warm.

Spiced Tomato and Lentil Soup

Serves: 1 | Prep Time: 10 mins | Cook Time: 25 mins

Ingredients

- **Tomatoes (chopped)**: 2 medium
- **Red lentils (rinsed)**: ¼ cup
- **Vegetable broth**: 1 cup
- **Onion (chopped)**: ¼ medium
- **Garlic**: ½ clove
- **Olive oil**: 1 teaspoon
- **Ground cumin**: ¼ teaspoon
- **Salt**: To taste
- **Black pepper**: To taste

Instructions

1. **Sauté Aromatics**: Heat **olive oil** in a small pot over medium heat. Add **onion**, **garlic**, and **ground cumin**, cooking for 2–3 minutes.
2. **Add Lentils and Tomatoes**: Stir in the **lentils** and **chopped tomatoes**. Cook for 2 minutes.
3. **Simmer**: Add the **vegetable broth** and bring to a boil. Reduce heat and simmer for 20 minutes until the lentils are tender.
4. **Season and Serve**: Adjust seasoning with **salt** and **pepper**. Serve warm.

Benefits of Tomato Soups

Benefit	Why It's Great
Rich in Vitamin C	Tomatoes are a great source of vitamin C, helping to boost your immune system and keep your skin healthy during summer.
Hydrating	With their high water content, tomatoes help keep you hydrated, which is essential during hot summer days.
Antioxidant-Rich	Tomatoes are packed with lycopene, an antioxidant that protects your skin from harmful UV rays and reduces the signs of aging.
Low-Calorie	A low-calorie food, tomato soup is a refreshing option that fills you up without weighing you down on hot days.
Promotes Heart Health	Tomatoes help maintain healthy blood pressure and circulation due to their potassium and lycopene content, supporting overall heart health.

Zucchini

Chilled Zucchini and Dill Soup

Serves: 1 | Prep Time: 10 mins | Cook Time: 10 mins + Chill Time

Ingredients

- **Zucchini (sliced)**: ½ cup
- **Vegetable broth**: ½ cup
- **Plain yogurt**: ¼ cup
- **Garlic**: ½ clove
- **Fresh dill (chopped)**: ½ teaspoon
- **Olive oil**: 1 teaspoon
- **Salt**: To taste
- **Black pepper**: To taste
- **Optional garnish**: Dill sprigs

Instructions

1. **Cook the Zucchini**: Heat **olive oil** in a small pot over medium heat. Sauté **zucchini** and **garlic** for 3–4 minutes. Add **vegetable broth** and simmer for 5 minutes.
2. **Blend and Chill**: Blend the soup until smooth. Stir in **yogurt** and **dill**. Chill in the refrigerator for at least 1 hour.
3. **Season and Serve**: Adjust seasoning with **salt** and **pepper**. Garnish with fresh **dill sprigs** and serve cold.

Lemon Zucchini Soup

Serves: 1 | Prep Time: 10 mins | Cook Time: 20 mins

Ingredients

- **Zucchini (sliced)**: ¾ cup
- **Vegetable broth**: 1 cup
- **Lemon zest**: ½ teaspoon
- **Lemon juice**: ½ teaspoon
- **Garlic**: ½ clove
- **Olive oil**: 1 teaspoon
- **Salt**: To taste
- **Black pepper**: To taste
- **Optional garnish**: Lemon wedge

Instructions

1. **Sauté Aromatics**: Heat **olive oil** in a small pot over medium heat. Add **garlic** and cook for 1–2 minutes.
2. **Cook the Zucchini**: Add **zucchini** and sauté for 3 minutes. Pour in **vegetable broth** and bring to a boil. Reduce heat and simmer for 15 minutes.
3. **Blend and Add Lemon**: Blend the soup until smooth. Stir in **lemon zest** and **juice**.
4. **Season and Serve**: Adjust seasoning with **salt** and **pepper**. Garnish with a **lemon wedge**.

Creamy Zucchini and Basil Chowder

Serves: 1 | Prep Time: 10 mins | Cook Time: 25 mins

Ingredients

- **Zucchini (sliced)**: ¾ cup
- **Vegetable broth**: 1 cup
- **Whole milk or cream**: ¼ cup
- **Basil leaves**: 4 large
- **Garlic**: ½ clove
- **Olive oil**: 1 teaspoon
- **Salt**: To taste
- **Black pepper**: To taste
- **Optional garnish**: Basil sprig

Instructions

1. **Sauté Aromatics**: Heat **olive oil** in a small pot. Add **garlic** and sauté for 2–3 minutes.
2. **Cook Zucchini**: Add **zucchini** and cook for 3 minutes. Pour in **vegetable broth** and bring to a boil. Reduce heat and simmer for 15 minutes.
3. **Blend and Add Cream**: Blend the soup until smooth. Stir in **milk or cream** and **basil leaves**.
4. **Season and Serve**: Adjust seasoning with **salt** and **pepper**. Garnish with a fresh **basil sprig**.

Zucchini and Sweet Corn Soup

Serves: 1 | Prep Time: 10 mins | Cook Time: 20 mins

Ingredients

- **Zucchini (sliced):** ½ cup
- **Sweet corn kernels:** ½ cup
- **Vegetable broth:** 1 cup
- **Onion (chopped):** ¼ medium
- **Garlic:** ½ clove
- **Olive oil:** 1 teaspoon
- **Salt:** To taste
- **Black pepper:** To taste
- **Optional garnish:** Corn kernels

Instructions

1. **Sauté Aromatics:** Heat **olive oil** in a small pot over medium heat. Add **onion** and **garlic**, cooking for 3 minutes.
2. **Cook Vegetables:** Add **zucchini**, **corn**, and **vegetable broth**. Bring to a boil, then simmer for 15 minutes.
3. **Blend or Leave Chunky:** For a smooth soup, blend until creamy. For a chunky texture, leave as is.
4. **Season and Serve:** Adjust seasoning with **salt** and **pepper**. Garnish with extra **corn kernels**.

Benefits of Zucchini Soups

Benefit	Why It's Great
Low-Calorie	Zucchini is low in calories but high in nutrients, making it a great option for light summer meals without feeling heavy.
Hydrating	With a high water content, zucchini helps keep you hydrated during the hot summer months, promoting healthy skin and digestion.
Rich in Antioxidants	Zucchini contains antioxidants like vitamin C, which protect your cells from damage and promote overall wellness.
Supports Digestion	The fiber in zucchini aids digestion, helping maintain a healthy gut and regularity, especially during warmer weather.
Boosts Skin Health	Packed with vitamin A and C, zucchini supports skin health and helps combat dryness or irritation often caused by the sun.

Corn

Sweet Corn and Coconut Soup

Serves: 1 | Prep Time: 10 mins | Cook Time: 20 mins

Ingredients

- **Sweet corn kernels**: ½ cup
- **Coconut milk**: ½ cup
- **Vegetable broth**: 1 cup
- **Garlic**: ½ clove
- **Ginger (grated)**: ½ teaspoon
- **Olive oil**: 1 teaspoon
- **Lime juice**: ½ teaspoon
- **Salt**: To taste
- **Black pepper**: To taste
- **Optional garnish**: Cilantro

Instructions

1. **Sauté Aromatics**: Heat **olive oil** in a small pot. Add **garlic** and **ginger**, cooking for 1–2 minutes until fragrant.
2. **Cook the Corn**: Add the **sweet corn** and stir for 2 minutes. Pour in the **vegetable broth** and simmer for 10 minutes.
3. **Blend and Add Coconut Milk**: Blend the soup until smooth. Stir in the **coconut milk** and **lime juice**. Heat gently, but do not boil.
4. **Season and Serve**: Adjust seasoning with **salt** and **pepper**. Garnish with fresh **cilantro**, if desired.

Corn and Jalapeño Chowder

Serves: 1 | Prep Time: 10 mins | Cook Time: 25 mins

Ingredients

- **Sweet corn kernels**: ½ cup
- **Jalapeño (chopped)**: ¼ medium
- **Potato (diced)**: 1 small
- **Vegetable broth**: 1 cup
- **Onion (chopped)**: ¼ medium
- **Whole milk or cream**: ¼ cup
- **Olive oil**: 1 teaspoon
- **Salt**: To taste
- **Black pepper**: To taste
- **Optional garnish**: Chopped jalapeño

Instructions

1. **Sauté Aromatics**: Heat **olive oil** in a pot. Add **onion** and **jalapeño**, cooking for 3–4 minutes until softened.
2. **Cook the Vegetables**: Add the **corn** and **potato**. Pour in the **vegetable broth** and bring to a boil. Reduce heat and simmer for 15 minutes.
3. **Blend or Leave Chunky**: Blend half the soup for a creamy texture, leaving some corn and potato chunks intact. Stir in **milk or cream**.
4. **Season and Serve**: Adjust seasoning with **salt** and **pepper**. Garnish with chopped **jalapeño**, if desired.

Summer Corn and Tomato Stew

Serves: 1 | Prep Time: 10 mins | Cook Time: 30 mins

Ingredients

- **Sweet corn kernels**: ½ cup
- **Tomatoes (chopped)**: 1 medium
- **Zucchini (chopped)**: ¼ medium
- **Vegetable broth**: 1¼ cups
- **Garlic**: ½ clove
- **Olive oil**: 1 teaspoon
- **Salt**: To taste
- **Black pepper**: To taste
- **Optional garnish**: Basil leaves

Instructions

1. **Sauté Aromatics**: Heat **olive oil** in a small pot. Add **garlic** and cook for 1–2 minutes.
2. **Cook Vegetables**: Add **corn**, **tomatoes**, and **zucchini**. Stir and cook for 5 minutes.
3. **Simmer the Stew**: Add **vegetable broth** and simmer for 20 minutes until the vegetables are tender.
4. **Season and Serve**: Adjust seasoning with **salt** and **pepper**. Garnish with fresh **basil leaves**.

Grilled Corn and Black Bean Soup

Serves: 1 | Prep Time: 15 mins | Cook Time: 25 mins

Ingredients

- **Corn on the cob**: 1 ear
- **Black beans (canned)**: ½ cup
- **Vegetable broth**: 1 cup
- **Garlic**: ½ clove
- **Lime juice**: ½ teaspoon
- **Olive oil**: 1 teaspoon
- **Ground cumin**: ¼ teaspoon
- **Salt**: To taste
- **Black pepper**: To taste
- **Optional garnish**: Cilantro

Instructions

1. **Grill the Corn**: Remove husk and grill the **corn on the cob** over medium heat, turning occasionally, until slightly charred. Remove kernels with a knife.
2. **Sauté Aromatics**: Heat **olive oil** in a pot. Add **garlic** and **cumin**, cooking for 1–2 minutes.
3. **Simmer the Soup**: Add the **grilled corn**, **black beans**, and **vegetable broth**. Bring to a boil, then reduce heat and simmer for 15 minutes.
4. **Season and Serve**: Stir in **lime juice**, season with **salt** and **pepper**, and garnish with fresh **cilantro**.

Benefits of Corn Soups

Benefit	Why It's Great
Rich in Fiber	Corn is high in fiber, which supports digestion and helps keep you full during summer meals without feeling bloated.
Hydrating	With a high water content, corn helps keep you hydrated, which is essential during hot, sunny days.
Packed with Vitamins	Corn is a good source of vitamin C and B-vitamins, which help boost immunity and provide energy for outdoor summer activities.
Supports Heart Health	The fiber and antioxidants in corn help support heart health by reducing cholesterol levels and improving circulation.
Naturally Sweet	Corn adds a natural sweetness to soups, making them flavorful without the need for added sugars or artificial ingredients.

Cucumbers and Bell Peppers

Chilled Cucumber and Yogurt Soup

Serves: 1 | Prep Time: 10 mins | No Cook Time

Ingredients

- **Cucumber (peeled)**: ½ medium
- **Plain yogurt**: ¼ cup
- **Vegetable broth**: ½ cup
- **Garlic**: ½ clove
- **Fresh dill (chopped)**: ½ teaspoon
- **Olive oil**: 1 teaspoon
- **Salt**: To taste
- **Black pepper**: To taste
- **Optional garnish**: Dill sprigs

Instructions

1. **Blend Ingredients**: In a blender, combine **cucumber**, **yogurt**, **vegetable broth**, **garlic**, and **dill**. Blend until smooth.
2. **Chill**: Refrigerate for at least 30 minutes for flavors to meld.
3. **Season and Serve**: Adjust seasoning with **salt** and **pepper**. Garnish with fresh **dill sprigs** and serve cold.

Bell Pepper and Tomato Gazpacho

Serves: 1 | Prep Time: 15 mins | No Cook Time

Ingredients

- **Red bell pepper**: ½ medium
- **Tomatoes (ripe)**: 2 medium
- **Cucumber (peeled)**: ¼ medium
- **Garlic**: ½ clove
- **Olive oil**: 1 teaspoon
- **Red wine vinegar**: ½ teaspoon
- **Salt**: To taste
- **Black pepper**: To taste
- **Optional garnish**: Basil sprig

Instructions

1. **Blend Ingredients**: In a blender, combine **bell pepper**, **tomatoes**, **cucumber**, **garlic**, **olive oil**, and **red wine vinegar**. Blend until smooth.
2. **Chill**: Refrigerate for at least 1 hour before serving.
3. **Serve and Garnish**: Pour into a bowl and garnish with a fresh **basil sprig**.

Cucumber, Mint, and Lime Soup

Serves: 1 | Prep Time: 10 mins | No Cook Time

Ingredients

- **Cucumber (peeled)**: ½ medium
- **Fresh mint leaves**: 4 large
- **Lime juice**: ½ teaspoon
- **Vegetable broth**: ½ cup
- **Olive oil**: 1 teaspoon
- **Salt**: To taste
- **Black pepper**: To taste
- **Optional garnish**: Mint sprig

Instructions

1. **Blend Ingredients**: In a blender, combine **cucumber**, **mint leaves**, **lime juice**, **vegetable broth**, and **olive oil**. Blend until smooth.
2. **Chill**: Refrigerate for at least 30 minutes.
3. **Season and Serve**: Adjust seasoning with **salt** and **pepper**. Garnish with a fresh **mint sprig**.

Roasted Red Pepper and Cucumber Soup

Serves: 1 | Prep Time: 10 mins | Cook Time: 20 mins

Ingredients

- **Red bell pepper**: 1 medium
- **Cucumber (peeled)**: ½ medium
- **Vegetable broth**: 1 cup
- **Garlic**: ½ clove
- **Olive oil**: 1 teaspoon
- **Salt**: To taste
- **Black pepper**: To taste
- **Optional garnish**: Basil sprig

Instructions

1. **Roast the Bell Pepper**: Preheat the oven to 400°F (200°C). Roast the **bell pepper** for 15–20 minutes, turning occasionally, until the skin is charred. Peel and chop.
2. **Blend Ingredients**: In a blender, combine **roasted bell pepper**, **cucumber**, **garlic**, and **vegetable broth**. Blend until smooth.
3. **Season and Serve**: Adjust seasoning with **salt** and **pepper**. Garnish with a fresh **basil sprig** and serve chilled or warm.

Benefits of Cucumber and Bell Pepper Soups

Benefit	Why It's Great
Hydrating	Both cucumbers and bell peppers have high water content, helping keep you hydrated during hot summer days.
Low-Calorie	These vegetables are naturally low in calories, making them perfect for light, refreshing summer soups.
Rich in Vitamin C	Bell peppers, especially red ones, are packed with vitamin C, boosting your immune system and supporting healthy skin.
Supports Digestion	The fiber in cucumbers and bell peppers promotes healthy digestion and keeps your gut happy during warmer weather.
Promotes Skin Health	With antioxidants and vitamins, these vegetables help maintain a healthy, glowing complexion in the summer sun.

Tip: Add fresh herbs like mint or basil to enhance the refreshing flavors of this light summer soup!

Watermelon

Watermelon Mint Gazpacho

Serves: 1 | Prep Time: 10 mins | No Cook Time

Ingredients

- **Watermelon (cubed)**: 1 cup
- **Cucumber (peeled)**: ¼ medium
- **Lime juice**: ½ teaspoon
- **Fresh mint leaves**: 4 large
- **Olive oil**: 1 teaspoon
- **Salt**: To taste
- **Optional garnish**: Mint sprigs

Instructions

1. **Blend Ingredients**: In a blender, combine **watermelon**, **cucumber**, **lime juice**, **mint leaves**, and **olive oil**. Blend until smooth.
2. **Chill**: Refrigerate for at least 30 minutes for flavors to meld.
3. **Season and Serve**: Adjust seasoning with **salt**. Garnish with fresh **mint sprigs** and serve cold.

Chilled Watermelon and Basil Soup

Serves: 1 | Prep Time: 10 mins | No Cook Time

Ingredients

- **Watermelon (cubed)**: 1 cup
- **Basil leaves**: 4 large
- **Lime juice**: ½ teaspoon
- **Olive oil**: 1 teaspoon
- **Salt**: To taste
- **Black pepper**: To taste
- **Optional garnish**: Basil sprigs

Instructions

1. **Blend Ingredients**: Combine **watermelon**, **basil leaves**, **lime juice**, and **olive oil** in a blender. Blend until smooth.
2. **Chill**: Refrigerate for at least 30 minutes.
3. **Season and Serve**: Adjust seasoning with **salt** and **pepper**. Garnish with a **basil sprig** and serve cold.

Watermelon and Cucumber Fusion Soup

Serves: 1 | Prep Time: 10 mins | No Cook Time

Ingredients

- **Watermelon (cubed)**: 1 cup
- **Cucumber (peeled)**: ½ medium
- **Lime juice**: ½ teaspoon
- **Fresh mint leaves**: 4 large
- **Olive oil**: 1 teaspoon
- **Salt**: To taste
- **Black pepper**: To taste
- **Optional garnish**: Mint sprig

Instructions

1. **Blend Ingredients**: In a blender, combine **watermelon**, **cucumber**, **lime juice**, **mint leaves**, and **olive oil**. Blend until smooth.
2. **Chill**: Refrigerate for at least 30 minutes.
3. **Season and Serve**: Adjust seasoning with **salt** and **pepper**. Garnish with a **mint sprig** and serve cold.

Watermelon, Tomato, and Chili Soup

Serves: 1 | Prep Time: 10 mins | No Cook Time

Ingredients

- **Watermelon (cubed)**: 1 cup
- **Tomato (chopped)**: ½ medium
- **Red chili (seeded)**: ¼ medium
- **Lime juice**: ½ teaspoon
- **Olive oil**: 1 teaspoon
- **Salt**: To taste
- **Optional garnish**: Chili flakes

Instructions

1. **Blend Ingredients**: In a blender, combine **watermelon**, **tomato**, **red chili**, **lime juice**, and **olive oil**. Blend until smooth.
2. **Chill**: Refrigerate for at least 30 minutes.
3. **Season and Serve**: Adjust seasoning with **salt**. Garnish with **chili flakes** for a spicy kick.

Benefits of Watermelon Soups

Benefit	Why It's Great
Highly Hydrating	Watermelon is made up of over 90% water, making it an excellent choice for staying hydrated on hot summer days.
Low-Calorie	Naturally low in calories, watermelon soup is a refreshing, guilt-free option for summer snacking.
Rich in Antioxidants	Packed with lycopene, an antioxidant that helps protect the skin from UV damage and reduce inflammation.
Supports Heart Health	Watermelon contains citrulline, which helps improve blood flow and supports healthy heart function.
Refreshing and Energizing	The natural sugars in watermelon provide a quick energy boost, perfect for an afternoon pick-me-up during warm weather.

Tip: Add a splash of lime or fresh mint for extra zest and freshness!

Eggplant

Smoky Eggplant and Tomato Soup

Serves: 1 | Prep Time: 15 mins | Cook Time: 35 mins

Ingredients

- **Eggplant (medium)**: 1
- **Tomato (chopped, medium)**: 1
- **Garlic (minced)**: 1 clove
- **Vegetable broth**: 1 cup
- **Olive oil**: 1 teaspoon
- **Smoked paprika**: ½ teaspoon
- **Salt**: To taste
- **Black pepper**: To taste
- **Optional garnish**: Fresh parsley

Instructions

1. **Roast the Eggplant**: Preheat the oven to 400°F (200°C). Pierce the **eggplant** with a fork and roast on a baking sheet for 25–30 minutes until soft. Peel and set aside.
2. **Cook the Aromatics**: Heat **olive oil** in a pot over medium heat. Add **garlic** and cook for 1–2 minutes.
3. **Combine Ingredients**: Add the **roasted eggplant**, **tomato**, **vegetable broth**, and **smoked paprika**. Simmer for 10 minutes.
4. **Blend and Season**: Blend the soup until smooth. Adjust seasoning with **salt** and **pepper**.
5. **Serve and Garnish**: Ladle into a bowl and garnish with fresh **parsley**, if desired.

Roasted Eggplant and Garlic Soup

Serves: 1 | Prep Time: 10 mins | Cook Time: 30 mins

Ingredients

- **Eggplant (cubed, medium)**: 1
- **Garlic**: 1 clove
- **Onion (chopped, small)**: 1
- **Vegetable broth**: 1 cup
- **Olive oil**: 1 teaspoon
- **Ground cumin**: ½ teaspoon
- **Salt**: To taste
- **Black pepper**: To taste
- **Optional garnish**: Croutons

Instructions

1. **Roast the Vegetables**: Preheat the oven to 400°F (200°C). Toss **eggplant** and **garlic** with **olive oil**, **salt**, and **pepper**. Roast for 20 minutes until golden.
2. **Sauté the Onion**: Heat **olive oil** in a pot over medium heat. Add the **onion** and cook for 3–4 minutes until softened.
3. **Simmer the Soup**: Add the roasted **eggplant** and **garlic**, along with the **vegetable broth** and **ground cumin**. Simmer for 10 minutes.
4. **Blend and Serve**: Blend the soup until smooth.

Eggplant and Red Lentil Stew

Serves: 1 | Prep Time: 15 mins | Cook Time: 30 mins

Ingredients

- **Eggplant (cubed, medium)**: ½
- **Red lentils (rinsed)**: ¼ cup
- **Onion (chopped, small)**: ½
- **Garlic (minced)**: 1 clove
- **Olive oil**: 1 teaspoon
- **Vegetable broth**: 1 cup
- **Ground turmeric**: ½ teaspoon
- **Ground cumin**: ½ teaspoon
- **Salt**: To taste
- **Black pepper**: To taste
- **Optional garnish**: Fresh cilantro

Instructions

1. **Sauté Aromatics**: Heat **olive oil** in a pot over medium heat. Add **onion**, **garlic**, **turmeric**, and **cumin**. Cook for 2–3 minutes until fragrant.
2. **Add Eggplant and Lentils**: Stir in the **eggplant** and **red lentils**. Cook for 2 minutes.
3. **Simmer the Stew**: Add the **vegetable broth** and bring to a boil. Reduce heat and simmer for 20–25 minutes until the lentils and eggplant are tender.
4. **Season and Serve**: Season with salt and pepper. Garnish with cilantro.

Eggplant and Tahini Soup

Serves: 1 | Prep Time: 10 mins | Cook Time: 25 mins

Ingredients

- **Eggplant (cubed, medium)**: 1
- **Onion (chopped, small)**: 1
- **Garlic (minced)**: 1 clove
- **Vegetable broth**: 1 cup
- **Olive oil**: 1 teaspoon
- **Tahini**: 1 tablespoon
- **Ground coriander**: ½ teaspoon
- **Salt**: To taste
- **Black pepper**: To taste
- **Optional garnish**: Lemon wedges

Instructions

1. **Sauté the Vegetables**: Heat **olive oil** in a pot. Add **eggplant**, **onion**, and **garlic**, cooking for 5 minutes until softened.
2. **Simmer the Soup**: Add the **vegetable broth** and **coriander**. Bring to a boil, then simmer for 15 minutes.
3. **Blend and Add Tahini**: Blend the soup until smooth. Stir in the **tahini** and adjust seasoning with **salt** and **pepper**.
4. **Serve and Garnish**: Serve with a wedge of **lemon** for a zesty touch.

Benefits of Eggplant Soups

Benefit	Why It's Great
Low-Calorie	Eggplants are low in calories but high in fiber, making them perfect for light summer meals that keep you full longer.
Rich in Antioxidants	Packed with anthocyanins, eggplant helps protect your cells from free radicals and reduces inflammation.
Supports Digestion	The fiber in eggplant aids digestion and promotes gut health, which is especially important in the summer heat.
Hydrating	Eggplants have a high water content, helping to keep you hydrated during warm summer days.
Promotes Heart Health	Rich in potassium and fiber, eggplants help regulate blood pressure and improve cholesterol levels.

Tip: Add garlic, olive oil, or fresh herbs like basil to bring out the savory, smoky flavor of eggplant in your soup!

Green Beans

Green Bean and Tomato Broth

Serves: 1 | Prep Time: 10 mins | Cook Time: 20 mins

Ingredients

- **Green beans (trimmed and chopped)**: ½ cup
- **Tomato (chopped, medium)**: 1
- **Garlic (minced)**: 1 clove
- **Olive oil**: 1 teaspoon
- **Vegetable broth**: 1 cup
- **Salt**: To taste
- **Black pepper**: To taste
- **Optional garnish**: Fresh parsley

Instructions

1. **Sauté the Garlic**: Heat **olive oil** in a pot over medium heat. Add **garlic** and sauté for 1–2 minutes.
2. **Add Tomato and Green Beans**: Stir in the **tomato** and **green beans**. Cook for 5 minutes.
3. **Simmer the Broth**: Add **vegetable broth** and simmer for 10–15 minutes until the green beans are tender.
4. **Season and Serve**: Adjust seasoning with **salt** and **pepper**. Garnish with fresh **parsley** and serve warm.

Green Bean and Sweet Corn Soup

Serves: 1 | Prep Time: 10 mins | Cook Time: 20 mins

Ingredients

- **Green beans (trimmed and chopped)**: ½ cup
- **Sweet corn kernels**: ½ cup
- **Onion (chopped, medium)**: ¼
- **Garlic (minced)**: 1 clove
- **Olive oil**: 1 teaspoon
- **Vegetable broth**: 1 cup
- **Salt**: To taste
- **Black pepper**: To taste
- **Optional garnish**: Croutons

Instructions

1. **Sauté the Aromatics**: Heat **olive oil** in a pot. Add **onion** and **garlic**, cooking for 2–3 minutes until softened.
2. **Add Vegetables**: Stir in **green beans** and **sweet corn**, cooking for 3 minutes.
3. **Simmer the Soup**: Add **vegetable broth** and simmer for 10–15 minutes until the green beans are tender.
4. **Season and Serve**: Adjust seasoning with **salt** and **pepper**. Garnish with croutons if desired.

Green Bean and Basil Stew

Serves: 1 | Prep Time: 15 mins | Cook Time: 25 mins

Ingredients

- **Green beans (trimmed and chopped)**: ½ cup
- **Onion (chopped, medium)**: ¼
- **Garlic (minced)**: 1 clove
- **Tomato (chopped, medium)**: 1
- **Vegetable broth**: 1 cup
- **Basil leaves (large)**: 4
- **Olive oil**: 1 teaspoon
- **Salt**: To taste
- **Black pepper**: To taste
- **Optional garnish**: Fresh basil

Instructions

1. **Sauté Aromatics**: Heat **olive oil** in a pot over medium heat. Add **onion** and **garlic**, cooking for 2–3 minutes.
2. **Add Vegetables**: Stir in the **green beans** and **tomato**, cooking for 5 minutes.
3. **Simmer the Stew**: Add **vegetable broth** and simmer for 15 minutes until the green beans are tender. Stir in **basil leaves** during the last 2 minutes of cooking.
4. **Season and Serve**: Adjust seasoning with **salt** and **pepper**. Garnish with fresh **basil**.

Creamy Green Bean and Potato Soup

Serves: 1 | Prep Time: 10 mins | Cook Time: 25 mins

Ingredients

- **Green beans (trimmed and chopped)**: ½ cup
- **Potato (diced, small)**: 1
- **Onion (chopped, medium)**: ¼
- **Garlic (minced)**: 1 clove
- **Olive oil**: 1 teaspoon
- **Vegetable broth**: 1 cup
- **Whole milk or cream**: ¼ cup
- **Salt**: To taste
- **Black pepper**: To taste
- **Optional garnish**: Fresh parsley

Instructions

1. **Sauté the Vegetables**: Heat **olive oil** in a pot. Add **onion**, **garlic**, and **potato**, cooking for 5 minutes.
2. **Add Green Beans and Broth**: Stir in the **green beans** and **vegetable broth**. Bring to a boil, then simmer for 15 minutes until the potatoes and green beans are tender.
3. **Blend and Add Cream**: Blend the soup until smooth. Stir in the **milk or cream**. Heat gently but do not boil.
4. **Season and Serve**: Adjust seasoning with **salt** and **pepper**. Garnish with fresh **parsley**.

Benefits of Green Bean Soups

Benefit	Why It's Great
Low-Calorie	Green beans are low in calories but high in fiber, making them perfect for light summer meals that still satisfy.
Rich in Vitamins	Packed with vitamin C, green beans support immune health and help protect your skin from summer sun damage.
Hydrating	With a high water content, green beans help keep you hydrated during hot summer days.
Supports Digestion	The fiber in green beans promotes healthy digestion and helps maintain a balanced gut.
Rich in Antioxidants	Green beans contain antioxidants that help reduce inflammation and support overall health.

Tip: Enhance the flavor with fresh herbs like thyme or a squeeze of lemon to bring out the natural freshness of green beans!

Fall: Cozy and Hearty
Pumpkin

Roasted Pumpkin and Sage Soup

Serves: 1 | Prep Time: 10 mins | Cook Time: 30 mins

Ingredients

- **Pumpkin (cubed)**: ½ cup
- **Garlic (whole)**: 1 clove
- **Olive oil**: 1 teaspoon
- **Vegetable broth**: 1 cup
- **Fresh sage leaves**: 2
- **Whole milk or cream**: ¼ cup
- **Salt**: To taste
- **Black pepper**: To taste
- **Optional garnish**: Toasted pumpkin seeds

Instructions

1. **Roast the Pumpkin**: Preheat oven to 400°F (200°C). Toss **pumpkin** and **garlic** with **olive oil**, and roast on a baking sheet for 20–25 minutes until golden and tender.

2. **Simmer with Sage**: In a pot, add the roasted **pumpkin**, **garlic**, **vegetable broth**, and **sage leaves**. Simmer for 5 minutes.

3. **Blend and Add Cream**: Blend the soup until smooth. Stir in the **milk or cream**, and season with **salt** and **pepper**.

4. **Serve and Garnish**: Serve warm and garnish with toasted **pumpkin seeds**, if desired.

Pumpkin and Coconut Stew

Serves: 1 | Prep Time: 10 mins | Cook Time: 25 mins

Ingredients

- **Pumpkin (cubed)**: ½ cup
- **Sweet potato (cubed)**: ¼ cup
- **Garlic (minced)**: 1 clove
- **Ginger (grated)**: ½ teaspoon
- **Coconut milk**: 1 cup
- **Vegetable broth**: ½ cup
- **Ground turmeric**: ½ teaspoon
- **Salt**: To taste
- **Black pepper**: To taste
- **Optional garnish**: Fresh cilantro

Instructions

1. **Sauté Aromatics**: Heat **olive oil** in a pot. Add **garlic**, **ginger**, and **turmeric**, cooking for 1–2 minutes until fragrant.
2. **Add Vegetables**: Stir in **pumpkin** and **sweet potato**. Cook for 3 minutes.
3. **Simmer the Stew**: Add **coconut milk** and **vegetable broth**. Simmer for 15–20 minutes until the vegetables are tender.
4. **Season and Serve**: Season to taste. Garnish with cilantro

---

Smoky Pumpkin Chili

Serves: 1 | Prep Time: 10 mins | Cook Time: 30 mins

Ingredients

- ½ cup **pumpkin (cubed)**
- ¼ cup **black beans (cooked)**
- ¼ cup **tomatoes (chopped)**
- 1 clove **garlic (minced)**
- 1 teaspoon **olive oil**
- ½ teaspoon **smoked paprika**
- ½ teaspoon **ground cumin**
- 1 cup **vegetable broth**
- **Salt and black pepper** to taste
- Optional: Sour cream for garnish

Instructions

1. **Sauté Aromatics**: Heat **olive oil** in a pot. Add **garlic**, **paprika**, and **cumin**, cooking for 1–2 minutes.
2. **Add Pumpkin and Tomatoes**: Stir in **pumpkin** and **tomatoes**, cooking for 5 minutes.
3. **Simmer the Chili**: Add **black beans** and **vegetable broth**. Simmer for 20 minutes until the pumpkin is tender and the chili is thickened.
4. **Season and Serve**: Season to taste. Add sour cream if desired.

Pumpkin and Lentil Soup

Serves: 1 | Prep Time: 10 mins | Cook Time: 30 mins

Ingredients

- **Pumpkin (cubed)**: ½ cup
- **Red lentils (rinsed)**: ¼ cup
- **Onion (chopped, medium)**: ¼
- **Garlic (minced)**: 1 clove
- **Olive oil**: 1 teaspoon
- **Vegetable broth**: 1 cup
- **Ground coriander**: ½ teaspoon
- **Salt**: To taste
- **Black pepper**: To taste
- **Optional garnish**: Fresh parsley

Instructions

1. **Sauté Aromatics**: Heat **olive oil** in a pot. Add **onion**, **garlic**, and **coriander**, cooking for 2–3 minutes.
2. **Add Pumpkin and Lentils**: Stir in **pumpkin** and **lentils**. Cook for 2 minutes.
3. **Simmer the Soup**: Add **vegetable broth** and bring to a boil. Reduce heat and simmer for 20–25 minutes until the lentils and pumpkin are tender.
4. **Blend and Serve**: Blend the soup partially for a chunky texture or until smooth. Season with **salt** and **pepper**. Garnish with fresh **parsley**.

Benefits of Pumpkin Soups

Benefit	Why It's Great
Rich in Vitamin A	Pumpkin is packed with beta-carotene, which supports eye health and boosts your immune system during the fall.
High in Fiber	The fiber in pumpkin helps with digestion, keeps you full longer, and supports gut health as the weather cools.
Supports Skin Health	The vitamin A and antioxidants in pumpkin promote healthy, glowing skin, especially as the weather dries out skin.
Boosts Immunity	Rich in vitamins A, C, and E, pumpkin helps strengthen the immune system during cold and flu season.
Low-Calorie & Filling	Low in calories but high in nutrients, pumpkin soup is a hearty yet light option for fall meals.

Butternut Squash

Butternut Squash and Apple Bisque

Serves: 1 | Prep Time: 10 mins | Cook Time: 25 mins

Ingredients

- **Butternut squash (cubed)**: ½ cup
- **Apple (peeled and chopped, medium)**: ¼
- **Onion (chopped, medium)**: ¼
- **Garlic (minced)**: 1 clove
- **Vegetable broth**: 1 cup
- **Whole milk or cream**: ¼ cup
- **Ground nutmeg**: ½ teaspoon
- **Olive oil**: 1 teaspoon
- **Salt**: To taste
- **Black pepper**: To taste
- **Optional garnish**: Apple slices

Instructions

1. **Sauté the Aromatics**: Heat **olive oil** in a pot over medium heat. Add **onion**, **garlic**, and **nutmeg**, and sauté for 2–3 minutes until fragrant.
2. **Cook Squash and Apple**: Add the **butternut squash** and **apple** to the pot. Cook for 5 minutes.
3. **Simmer the Bisque**: Add the **vegetable broth** and simmer for 15 minutes until the squash is tender.
4. **Blend and Add Cream**: Blend the soup until smooth. Stir in **milk or cream** and season with **salt** and **pepper**.
5. **Serve and Garnish**: Garnish with thin **apple slices** if desired.

Creamy Squash and Cinnamon Soup

Serves: 1 | Prep Time: 10 mins | Cook Time: 25 mins

Ingredients

- **Butternut squash (cubed)**: ½ cup
- **Onion (chopped, medium)**: ¼
- **Garlic (minced)**: 1 clove
- **Vegetable broth**: 1 cup
- **Coconut milk**: ¼ cup
- **Ground cinnamon**: ½ teaspoon
- **Olive oil**: 1 teaspoon
- **Salt**: To taste
- **Black pepper**: To taste
- **Optional garnish**: Cinnamon stick

Instructions

1. **Sauté Aromatics**: Heat **olive oil** in a pot. Add **onion**, **garlic**, and **cinnamon**, cooking for 2–3 minutes.
2. **Cook Squash**: Add **butternut squash** and cook for 5 minutes.
3. **Simmer the Soup**: Add **vegetable broth** and simmer for 15–20 minutes until the squash is tender.
4. **Blend and Add Coconut Milk**: Blend the soup until smooth. Stir in **coconut milk** and season with **salt** and **pepper**.
5. **Serve and Garnish**: Garnish with a **cinnamon stick**, if desired.

Roasted Butternut and Ginger Stew

Serves: 1 | Prep Time: 10 mins | Cook Time: 30 mins

Ingredients

- **Butternut squash (cubed)**: ½ cup
- **Ginger (grated)**: ½ teaspoon
- **Onion (chopped, medium)**: ¼
- **Garlic (minced)**: 1 clove
- **Olive oil**: 1 teaspoon
- **Vegetable broth**: 1 cup
- **Ground turmeric**: ½ teaspoon
- **Salt**: To taste
- **Black pepper**: To taste
- **Optional garnish**: Fresh cilantro

Instructions

1. **Roast the Squash**: Preheat oven to 400°F (200°C). Toss **butternut squash** with **olive oil**, and roast on a baking sheet for 20 minutes until caramelized.
2. **Sauté Aromatics**: Heat **olive oil** in a pot. Add **onion**, **garlic**, **ginger**, and **turmeric**, cooking for 2–3 minutes.
3. **Simmer the Stew**: Add the roasted **butternut squash** and **vegetable broth**. Simmer for 10 minutes.
4. **Season and Serve**: Season with salt and pepper. Garnish with cilantro.

Butternut Squash and Sage Chowder

Serves: 1 | Prep Time: 10 mins | Cook Time: 30 mins

Ingredients

- **Butternut squash (cubed)**: ½ cup
- **Potato (diced, medium)**: ¼
- **Garlic (minced)**: 1 clove
- **Olive oil**: 1 teaspoon
- **Vegetable broth**: 1 cup
- **Whole milk or cream**: ¼ cup
- **Fresh sage leaves**: 2
- **Salt**: To taste
- **Black pepper**: To taste
- **Optional garnish**: Croutons

Instructions

1. **Sauté Aromatics**: Heat **olive oil** in a pot. Add **garlic** and **sage leaves**, and sauté for 1–2 minutes until fragrant.
2. **Cook Vegetables**: Add **butternut squash** and **potato**. Cook for 5 minutes.
3. **Simmer the Chowder**: Add **vegetable broth** and simmer for 20 minutes until the vegetables are tender.
4. **Blend and Add Cream**: Blend the soup until smooth. Stir in **milk or cream**, and season with **salt** and **pepper**.
5. **Serve and Garnish**: Garnish with croutons if desired.

Benefits of Butternut Squash Soups

Benefit	Why It's Great
Rich in Vitamin A	Butternut squash is high in beta-carotene, which supports eye health and boosts immunity, especially in fall.
High in Fiber	The fiber in butternut squash aids digestion and helps keep you full, perfect for a cozy fall meal.
Supports Skin Health	Packed with vitamins A and C, it promotes healthy skin and helps combat dryness that often comes with cooler weather.
Rich in Antioxidants	Butternut squash contains antioxidants that reduce inflammation and fight free radicals, supporting overall health.
Low-Calorie & Nutritious	A low-calorie option that is still nutrient-dense, providing a filling, healthy meal during the fall season.

Tip: Add a dash of cinnamon or a swirl of cream for extra warmth and richness in your butternut squash soup!

Sweet Potatoes

Sweet Potato and Carrot Soup

Serves: 1 | Prep Time: 10 mins | Cook Time: 25 mins

Ingredients

- **Sweet potato**: ½ cup (cubed)
- **Carrot**: ½ cup (sliced)
- **Garlic**: 1 clove (minced)
- **Onion**: ¼ medium (chopped)
- **Olive oil**: 1 teaspoon
- **Vegetable broth**: 1 cup
- **Ground ginger**: ½ teaspoon
- **Salt and black pepper**: To taste
- **Optional garnish**: Fresh parsley

Instructions

1. **Sauté Aromatics**: Heat **olive oil** in a pot over medium heat. Add **onion**, **garlic**, and **ginger**, and cook for 2–3 minutes until fragrant.
2. **Cook Vegetables**: Add **sweet potato** and **carrot**. Stir well and cook for 3 minutes.
3. **Simmer the Soup**: Pour in **vegetable broth** and simmer for 15–20 minutes until the vegetables are tender.
4. **Blend and Season**: Blend the soup until smooth. Adjust seasoning with **salt** and **pepper**.
5. **Serve and Garnish**: Garnish with fresh **parsley** if desired.

Spiced Sweet Potato Stew

Serves: 1 | Prep Time: 10 mins | Cook Time: 30 mins

Ingredients

- **Sweet potato**: ½ cup (cubed)
- **Chickpeas**: ¼ cup (cooked)
- **Garlic**: 1 clove (minced)
- **Onion**: ¼ medium (chopped)
- **Olive oil**: 1 teaspoon
- **Vegetable broth**: 1 cup
- **Ground cumin**: ½ teaspoon
- **Ground coriander**: ½ teaspoon
- **Salt and black pepper**: To taste
- **Optional garnish**: Lemon wedge

Instructions

1. **Sauté Aromatics**: Heat **olive oil** in a pot. Add **onion**, **garlic**, **cumin**, and **coriander**, cooking for 2–3 minutes.
2. **Add Sweet Potato and Chickpeas**: Stir in **sweet potato** and **chickpeas**, cooking for 3 minutes.
3. **Simmer the Stew**: Add **vegetable broth** and simmer for 20–25 minutes until the sweet potato is tender.
4. **Season and Serve**: Adjust seasoning with **salt** and **pepper**. Garnish with a **lemon wedge**.

Sweet Potato and Black Bean Chili

Serves: 1 | Prep Time: 10 mins | Cook Time: 30 mins

Ingredients

- **Sweet potato**: ½ cup (cubed)
- **Black beans**: ¼ cup (cooked)
- **Tomatoes**: ¼ cup (chopped)
- **Garlic**: 1 clove (minced)
- **Olive oil**: 1 teaspoon
- **Vegetable broth**: 1 cup
- **Smoked paprika**: ½ teaspoon
- **Ground chili powder**: ½ teaspoon
- **Salt and black pepper**: To taste
- **Optional garnish**: Sour cream

Instructions

1. **Sauté Aromatics**: Heat **olive oil** in a pot. Add **garlic**, **smoked paprika**, and **chili powder**, cooking for 1–2 minutes.
2. **Add Vegetables and Beans**: Stir in **sweet potato**, **black beans**, and **tomatoes**. Cook for 5 minutes.

3. **Simmer the Chili**: Add **vegetable broth** and simmer for 20 minutes until the sweet potato is tender and the chili thickens.
4. **Season and Serve**: Adjust seasoning with **salt** and **pepper**. Garnish with a dollop of **sour cream** if desired.

Sweet Potato and Coconut Soup

Serves: 1 | Prep Time: 10 mins | Cook Time: 20 mins

Ingredients

- **Sweet potato**: ½ cup (cubed)
- **Garlic**: 1 clove (minced)
- **Ginger**: ½ teaspoon (grated)
- **Olive oil**: 1 teaspoon
- **Coconut milk**: ½ cup
- **Vegetable broth**: ½ cup
- **Ground turmeric**: ½ teaspoon
- **Salt and black pepper**: To taste
- **Optional garnish**: Fresh cilantro

Instructions

1. **Sauté Aromatics**: Heat **olive oil** in a pot. Add **garlic**, **ginger**, and **turmeric**, cooking for 1–2 minutes.
2. **Cook Sweet Potato**: Add **sweet potato** and cook for 5 minutes.
3. **Simmer the Soup**: Pour in **coconut milk** and **vegetable broth**. Simmer for 15 minutes until the sweet potato is tender.
4. **Blend and Serve**: Blend the soup until smooth. Adjust seasoning with **salt** and **pepper**. Garnish with fresh **cilantro**.

Benefits of Sweet Potato Soups

Benefit	Why It's Great
Rich in Vitamin A	Sweet potatoes are packed with beta-carotene, supporting eye health and boosting immunity during fall.
High in Fiber	The fiber content aids digestion and helps you feel full longer, making it a great comfort food for the season.
Supports Skin Health	The antioxidants and vitamins in sweet potatoes promote healthy, glowing skin as temperatures drop.
Promotes Heart Health	Rich in potassium, sweet potatoes help regulate blood pressure and support cardiovascular health.
Low Glycemic Index	Sweet potatoes have a low glycemic index, providing steady energy without causing blood sugar spikes.

Mushrooms

Mushroom and Barley Stew

Serves: 1 | Prep Time: 10 mins | Cook Time: 35 mins

Ingredients

- **Mushrooms**: ½ cup (sliced)
- **Barley**: ¼ cup
- **Onion**: ¼ medium (chopped)
- **Garlic**: 1 clove (minced)
- **Olive oil**: 1 teaspoon
- **Vegetable broth**: 1 cup
- **Fresh thyme**: ¼ teaspoon
- **Salt and black pepper**: To taste
- **Optional garnish**: Fresh parsley

Instructions

1. **Sauté Aromatics**: Heat **olive oil** in a pot over medium heat. Add **onion**, **garlic**, and **thyme**, cooking for 2–3 minutes.
2. **Cook Mushrooms**: Add **mushrooms** and sauté for 5 minutes until softened.
3. **Add Barley and Simmer**: Add **barley** and **vegetable broth**. Bring to a boil, then reduce heat and simmer for 25–30 minutes until the barley is tender.
4. **Season and Serve**: Adjust seasoning with **salt** and **pepper**. Garnish with fresh **parsley** if desired.

Creamy Mushroom Bisque

Serves: 1 | Prep Time: 10 mins | Cook Time: 25 mins

Ingredients

- **Mushrooms**: ½ cup (sliced)
- **Onion**: ¼ medium (chopped)
- **Garlic**: 1 clove (minced)
- **Olive oil**: 1 teaspoon
- **Vegetable broth**: 1 cup
- **Whole milk or cream**: ¼ cup
- **Ground nutmeg**: ¼ teaspoon
- **Salt and black pepper**: To taste
- **Optional garnish**: Croutons

Instructions

1. **Sauté Aromatics**: Heat **olive oil** in a pot over medium heat. Add **onion**, **garlic**, and **mushrooms**, and cook for 5 minutes until softened.
2. **Simmer the Soup**: Add **vegetable broth** and simmer for 15 minutes.
3. **Blend and Add Cream**: Blend the soup until smooth. Stir in **milk or cream** and **nutmeg**, heating gently without boiling.
4. **Season and Serve**: Adjust seasoning with **salt** and **pepper**. Garnish with croutons if desired.

Wild Mushroom and Thyme Soup

Serves: 1 | Prep Time: 10 mins | Cook Time: 30 mins

Ingredients

- **Wild mushrooms**: ½ cup (chopped)
- **Onion**: ¼ medium (chopped)
- **Garlic**: 1 clove (minced)
- **Olive oil**: 1 teaspoon
- **Vegetable broth**: 1 cup
- **Fresh thyme**: ¼ teaspoon
- **Salt and black pepper**: To taste
- **Optional garnish**: Thyme sprig

Instructions

1. **Sauté Aromatics**: Heat **olive oil** in a pot over medium heat. Add **onion**, **garlic**, and **thyme**, and sauté for 2–3 minutes.
2. **Cook Mushrooms**: Add **wild mushrooms** and cook for 5 minutes.
3. **Simmer the Soup**: Pour in **vegetable broth** and simmer for 20 minutes.
4. **Season and Serve**: Adjust seasoning with **salt** and **pepper**. Garnish with a thyme sprig if desired.

Porcini and Garlic Soup

Serves: 1 | Prep Time: 10 mins | Cook Time: 20 mins

Ingredients

- **Porcini mushrooms (dried)**: ¼ cup
- **Onion**: ¼ medium (chopped)
- **Garlic**: 1 clove (minced)
- **Olive oil**: 1 teaspoon
- **Vegetable broth**: 1 cup
- **Fresh parsley**: ½ teaspoon (chopped)
- **Salt and black pepper**: To taste
- **Optional garnish**: Crusty bread

Instructions

1. **Rehydrate Mushrooms**: Soak **porcini mushrooms** in warm water for 10 minutes. Drain and chop.
2. **Sauté Aromatics**: Heat **olive oil** in a pot. Add **onion** and **garlic**, cooking for 2–3 minutes.
3. **Simmer the Soup**: Add rehydrated **porcini mushrooms** and **vegetable broth**. Simmer for 15 minutes.
4. **Season and Serve**: Adjust seasoning with **salt** and **pepper**. Garnish with fresh **parsley** and serve with crusty bread.

Benefits of Mushroom Soups

Benefit	Why It's Great
Rich in Vitamin D	Mushrooms are one of the few plant sources of vitamin D, helping to boost immunity as the days get shorter.
Supports Immune Health	Packed with antioxidants and beta-glucans, mushrooms strengthen the immune system, making them perfect for fall.
Rich in Fiber	The fiber in mushrooms supports digestion and promotes gut health, especially helpful during the cooler months.
Low-Calorie & Nutritious	Low in calories but high in nutrients, mushrooms make a hearty yet light meal for the fall season.
Promotes Heart Health	Mushrooms contain compounds that help lower cholesterol and support overall heart health.

Tip: Add a splash of cream or a sprinkle of thyme to enhance the earthy flavors of mushroom soup!

Root Vegetables

Root Vegetable and Lentil Stew

Serves: 1 | Prep Time: 10 mins | Cook Time: 30 mins

Ingredients

- **Carrot**: ½ cup (chopped)
- **Parsnip**: ½ cup (chopped)
- **Turnip**: ¼ cup (chopped)
- **Red lentils**: ¼ cup (rinsed)
- **Onion**: ¼ medium (chopped)
- **Garlic**: 1 clove (minced)
- **Olive oil**: 1 teaspoon
- **Vegetable broth**: 1¼ cups
- **Ground cumin**: ½ teaspoon
- **Salt and black pepper**: To taste
- **Optional garnish**: Fresh parsley

Instructions

1. **Sauté Aromatics**: Heat **olive oil** in a pot over medium heat. Add **onion, garlic**, and **cumin**, cooking for 2–3 minutes until fragrant.
2. **Add Vegetables and Lentils**: Stir in **carrot, parsnip, turnip**, and **lentils**. Cook for 3 minutes.
3. **Simmer the Stew**: Add **vegetable broth** and simmer for 20–25 minutes until the vegetables and lentils are tender.
4. **Season and Serve**: Adjust seasoning with **salt** and **pepper**. Garnish with fresh **parsley**.

Parsnip and Carrot Soup

Serves: 1 | Prep Time: 10 mins | Cook Time: 25 mins

Ingredients

- **Parsnip**: ½ cup (chopped)
- **Carrot**: ½ cup (chopped)
- **Onion**: ¼ medium (chopped)
- **Garlic**: 1 clove (minced)
- **Olive oil**: 1 teaspoon
- **Vegetable broth**: 1 cup
- **Ground nutmeg**: ¼ teaspoon
- **Salt and black pepper**: To taste
- **Optional garnish**: Croutons

Instructions

1. **Sauté Aromatics**: Heat **olive oil** in a pot. Add **onion**, **garlic**, and **nutmeg**, and cook for 2–3 minutes.
2. **Cook Vegetables**: Add **parsnip** and **carrot**, stirring well. Cook for 5 minutes.
3. **Simmer the Soup**: Add **vegetable broth** and simmer for 15–20 minutes until the vegetables are tender.
4. **Blend and Serve**: Blend the soup until smooth. Adjust seasoning with **salt** and **pepper**. Garnish with croutons if desired.

Turnip and Potato Chowder

Serves: 1 | Prep Time: 10 mins | Cook Time: 25 mins

Ingredients

- **Turnip**: ½ cup (diced)
- **Potato**: ½ cup (diced)
- **Onion**: ¼ medium (chopped)
- **Garlic**: 1 clove (minced)
- **Olive oil**: 1 teaspoon
- **Vegetable broth**: 1 cup
- **Whole milk or cream**: ¼ cup
- **Salt and black pepper**: To taste
- **Optional garnish**: Fresh thyme

Instructions

1. **Sauté Aromatics**: Heat **olive oil** in a pot over medium heat. Add **onion** and **garlic**, and cook for 2–3 minutes.
2. **Cook Vegetables**: Add **turnip** and **potato**, stirring well. Cook for 5 minutes.
3. **Simmer the Chowder**: Add **vegetable broth** and simmer for 15 minutes until the vegetables are tender. Stir in **milk or cream**.
4. **Season and Serve**: Adjust seasoning with **salt** and **pepper**. Garnish with fresh **thyme**.

Roasted Beet and Parsnip Soup

Serves: 1 | Prep Time: 10 mins | Cook Time: 30 mins

Ingredients

- **Beets**: ½ cup (cubed)
- **Parsnip**: ½ cup (cubed)
- **Garlic**: 1 clove (whole)
- **Olive oil**: 1 teaspoon
- **Vegetable broth**: 1 cup
- **Fresh dill**: ½ teaspoon (chopped)
- **Salt and black pepper**: To taste
- **Optional garnish**: Dill sprig

Instructions

1. **Roast the Vegetables**: Preheat oven to 400°F (200°C). Toss **beets**, **parsnip**, and **garlic** with **olive oil**. Roast for 20–25 minutes until tender.
2. **Simmer the Soup**: Transfer the roasted vegetables to a pot. Add **vegetable broth** and simmer for 5 minutes.
3. **Blend and Serve**: Blend the soup until smooth. Adjust seasoning with **salt** and **pepper**. Garnish with fresh **dill**.

Benefits of Root Vegetable Soups

Benefit	Why It's Great
Rich in Nutrients	Root vegetables like carrots, parsnips, and turnips are packed with vitamins A, C, and K, boosting immunity during fall.
Supports Digestion	High in fiber, root vegetables help regulate digestion and keep you feeling full longer as the weather cools.
Packed with Antioxidants	Root vegetables are rich in antioxidants, which help reduce inflammation and protect your body from seasonal illnesses.
Boosts Heart Health	Many root vegetables are rich in potassium, which helps regulate blood pressure and supports overall cardiovascular health.
Hearty and Filling	Root vegetable soups are filling and comforting, providing warmth and nourishment for cold fall days.

Tip: Add warming spices like cinnamon, nutmeg, or ginger to bring out the natural sweetness and depth of flavor in root vegetable soups!

Apples

Apple and Onion Soup

Serves: 1 | Prep Time: 10 mins | Cook Time: 25 mins

Ingredients

- **Apple**: ½ medium (peeled and chopped)
- **Onion**: ½ medium (sliced)
- **Garlic**: 1 clove (minced)
- **Olive oil**: 1 teaspoon
- **Vegetable broth**: 1 cup
- **Thyme**: ¼ teaspoon (dried or fresh)
- **Salt and black pepper**: To taste
- **Optional garnish**: Croutons

Instructions

1. **Sauté Aromatics**: Heat **olive oil** in a pot over medium heat. Add **onion**, **garlic**, and **thyme**, and cook for 5 minutes until caramelized.
2. **Add Apple and Broth**: Stir in the **apple** and cook for 2 minutes. Add **vegetable broth** and bring to a boil.
3. **Simmer the Soup**: Reduce heat and simmer for 15 minutes until the apple and onion are tender.
4. **Blend and Serve**: Blend the soup until smooth. Adjust seasoning with **salt** and **pepper**. Garnish with croutons if desired.

Butternut and Apple Stew

Serves: 1 | Prep Time: 10 mins | Cook Time: 30 mins

Ingredients

- **Butternut squash**: ½ cup (cubed)
- **Apple**: ½ medium (peeled and chopped)
- **Onion**: ¼ medium (chopped)
- **Garlic**: 1 clove (minced)
- **Olive oil**: 1 teaspoon
- **Vegetable broth**: 1¼ cups
- **Ground cinnamon**: ¼ teaspoon
- **Salt and black pepper**: To taste
- **Optional garnish**: Chopped parsley

Instructions

1. **Sauté Aromatics**: Heat **olive oil** in a pot. Add **onion**, **garlic**, and **cinnamon**, and cook for 2–3 minutes.
2. **Add Squash and Apple**: Stir in **butternut squash** and **apple**, cooking for 5 minutes.
3. **Simmer the Stew**: Add **vegetable broth** and simmer for 20–25 minutes until the squash is tender.
4. **Season and Serve**: Adjust seasoning with **salt** and **pepper**. Garnish with chopped parsley if desired.

Apple and Parsnip Cream Soup

Serves: 1 | Prep Time: 10 mins | Cook Time: 25 mins

Ingredients

- **Apple**: ½ medium (peeled and chopped)
- **Parsnip**: ½ cup (chopped)
- **Onion**: ¼ medium (chopped)
- **Garlic**: 1 clove (minced)
- **Olive oil**: 1 teaspoon
- **Vegetable broth**: 1 cup
- **Whole milk or cream**: ¼ cup
- **Ground nutmeg**: ¼ teaspoon
- **Salt and black pepper**: To taste
- **Optional garnish**: Crushed walnuts

Instructions

1. **Sauté Aromatics**: Heat **olive oil** in a pot. Add **onion**, **garlic**, and **nutmeg**, and cook for 2–3 minutes.
2. **Add Apple and Parsnip**: Stir in **apple** and **parsnip**, cooking for 5 minutes.
3. **Simmer the Soup**: Add **vegetable broth** and simmer for 15 minutes until the parsnip is tender.
4. **Blend and Add Cream**: Blend the soup until smooth. Stir in **milk or cream** and adjust seasoning with **salt** and **pepper**. Garnish with crushed walnuts.

Spiced Apple and Carrot Soup

Serves: 1 | Prep Time: 10 mins | Cook Time: 25 mins

Ingredients

- **Apple**: ½ medium (peeled and chopped)
- **Carrot**: ½ cup (sliced)
- **Onion**: ¼ medium (chopped)
- **Garlic**: 1 clove (minced)
- **Olive oil**: 1 teaspoon
- **Vegetable broth**: 1 cup
- **Ground cinnamon**: ¼ teaspoon
- **Ground ginger**: ¼ teaspoon
- **Salt and black pepper**: To taste
- **Optional garnish**: Apple slices

Instructions

1. **Sauté Aromatics**: Heat **olive oil** in a pot. Add **onion**, **garlic**, **cinnamon**, and **ginger**, cooking for 2–3 minutes.
2. **Add Apple and Carrot**: Stir in **apple** and **carrot**, cooking for 5 minutes.
3. **Simmer the Soup**: Add **vegetable broth** and simmer for 15–20 minutes until the carrot is tender.
4. **Blend and Serve**: Blend the soup until smooth. Adjust seasoning with **salt** and **pepper**. Garnish with thin **apple slices**.

Benefits of Apple Soups

Benefit	Why It's Great
Rich in Fiber	Apples are high in fiber, which supports digestion and keeps you feeling full longer, making them perfect for fall.
Boosts Immune Health	Packed with vitamin C, apples help strengthen the immune system during colder weather.
Supports Heart Health	Apples contain antioxidants and flavonoids that help lower cholesterol and support heart health.
Hydrating	With a high water content, apples help keep you hydrated as the weather cools down.
Natural Sweetness	Apples add a natural sweetness to soups, reducing the need for added sugars or artificial sweeteners.

Tip: Add a dash of cinnamon or a squeeze of lemon to enhance the fall flavors in your apple soup!

Cabbage

Cabbage and Sausage Stew

Serves: 1 | Prep Time: 10 mins | Cook Time: 30 mins

Ingredients

- **Cabbage**: ½ cup (shredded)
- **Sausage**: 1 small link (sliced)
- **Carrot**: ¼ cup (sliced)
- **Potato**: ¼ cup (diced)
- **Onion**: ¼ medium (chopped)
- **Garlic**: 1 clove (minced)
- **Olive oil**: 1 teaspoon
- **Vegetable broth**: 1¼ cups
- **Salt and black pepper**: To taste
- **Optional garnish**: Fresh parsley

Instructions

1. **Brown the Sausage**: Heat **olive oil** in a pot over medium heat. Add **sausage** slices and cook for 3–4 minutes until browned. Remove and set aside.
2. **Sauté Vegetables**: In the same pot, add **onion**, **garlic**, **carrot**, and **potato**, cooking for 5 minutes.
3. **Add Cabbage and Broth**: Stir in **cabbage** and **vegetable broth**. Simmer for 20 minutes.
4. **Combine and Serve**: Return the **sausage** to the pot. Season with **salt** and **pepper**. Garnish with fresh **parsley**.

Sweet and Sour Cabbage Soup

Serves: 1 | Prep Time: 10 mins | Cook Time: 25 mins

Ingredients

- **Cabbage**: ½ cup (shredded)
- **Tomato**: ½ medium (chopped)
- **Onion**: ¼ medium (chopped)
- **Garlic**: 1 clove (minced)
- **Apple cider vinegar**: ½ tablespoon
- **Brown sugar**: 1 teaspoon
- **Olive oil**: 1 teaspoon
- **Vegetable broth**: 1¼ cups
- **Salt and black pepper**: To taste
- **Optional garnish**: Fresh dill

Instructions

1. **Sauté Aromatics**: Heat **olive oil** in a pot. Add **onion** and **garlic**, cooking for 2–3 minutes.
2. **Add Cabbage and Tomato**: Stir in **cabbage** and **tomato**, cooking for 5 minutes.
3. **Simmer the Soup**: Add **vegetable broth**, **apple cider vinegar**, and **brown sugar**. Simmer for 15 minutes.
4. **Season and Serve**: Adjust seasoning with **salt** and **pepper**. Garnish with fresh **dill**.

Cabbage and White Bean Soup

Serves: 1 | Prep Time: 10 mins | Cook Time: 25 mins

Ingredients

- **Cabbage**: ½ cup (shredded)
- **White beans**: ¼ cup (cooked)
- **Carrot**: ¼ cup (sliced)
- **Onion**: ¼ medium (chopped)
- **Garlic**: 1 clove (minced)
- **Olive oil**: 1 teaspoon
- **Vegetable broth**: 1¼ cups
- **Salt and black pepper**: To taste
- **Optional garnish**: Parmesan

Instructions

1. **Sauté Aromatics**: Heat **olive oil** in a pot over medium heat. Add **onion**, **garlic**, and **carrot**, cooking for 3–4 minutes.
2. **Add Cabbage and Beans**: Stir in **cabbage** and **white beans**, cooking for 3 minutes.
3. **Simmer the Soup**: Add **vegetable broth** and simmer for 15–20 minutes until the cabbage is tender.
4. **Season and Serve**: Adjust seasoning with **salt** and **pepper**. Garnish with grated **Parmesan** if desired.

Cabbage and Root Vegetable Stew

Serves: 1 | Prep Time: 10 mins | Cook Time: 30 mins

Ingredients

- **Cabbage**: ½ cup (shredded)
- **Parsnip**: ¼ cup (chopped)
- **Turnip**: ¼ cup (chopped)
- **Potato**: ¼ cup (diced)
- **Onion**: ¼ medium (chopped)
- **Garlic**: 1 clove (minced)
- **Olive oil**: 1 teaspoon
- **Vegetable broth**: 1¼ cups
- **Fresh thyme**: ¼ teaspoon
- **Salt and black pepper**: To taste
- **Optional garnish**: Fresh thyme sprig

Instructions

1. **Sauté Aromatics**: Heat **olive oil** in a pot. Add **onion**, **garlic**, and **thyme**, and cook for 2–3 minutes.
2. **Add Vegetables**: Stir in **cabbage**, **parsnip**, **turnip**, and **potato**. Cook for 5 minutes.
3. **Simmer the Stew**: Add **vegetable broth** and simmer for 20–25 minutes until the vegetables are tender.
4. **Season and Serve**: Adjust seasoning with **salt** and **pepper**. Garnish with a sprig of **thyme**.

Benefits of Cabbage Soups

Benefit	Why It's Great
Rich in Vitamin C	Cabbage is packed with vitamin C, which supports the immune system during fall and helps fight off seasonal illnesses.
Supports Digestion	High in fiber, cabbage promotes healthy digestion and helps maintain a healthy gut, especially useful during fall.
Anti-Inflammatory	Cabbage contains anti-inflammatory compounds that can help reduce inflammation in the body, making it great for the colder months.
Boosts Heart Health	Rich in antioxidants and fiber, cabbage helps lower cholesterol levels and supports overall heart health.
Low-Calorie & Filling	Low in calories but filling, cabbage soup provides a nutritious and hearty option for fall meals without being heavy.

Brussels Sprouts

Roasted Brussels Sprouts and Potato Soup

Serves: 1 | Prep Time: 10 mins | Cook Time: 30 mins

Ingredients

- **Brussels sprouts**: ½ cup (halved)
- **Potato**: ½ cup (diced)
- **Garlic**: 1 clove (whole)
- **Onion**: ¼ medium (chopped)
- **Olive oil**: 1 teaspoon
- **Vegetable broth**: 1¼ cups
- **Salt and black pepper**: To taste
- **Optional garnish**: Croutons

Instructions

1. **Roast the Vegetables**: Preheat oven to 400°F (200°C). Toss **Brussels sprouts** and **garlic** with **olive oil**, and roast for 20 minutes until golden.
2. **Sauté the Onion**: Heat a small pot and sauté **onion** in a little oil for 3 minutes.
3. **Combine and Simmer**: Add roasted **Brussels sprouts**, **garlic**, and **potatoes** to the pot with **vegetable broth**. Simmer for 10 minutes.
4. **Blend and Serve**: Blend the soup until smooth. Season with **salt** and **pepper**. Garnish with croutons.

Creamy Brussels Sprouts Chowder

Serves: 1 | Prep Time: 10 mins | Cook Time: 25 mins

Ingredients

- **Brussels sprouts**: ½ cup (shredded)
- **Potato**: ¼ cup (diced)
- **Onion**: ¼ medium (chopped)
- **Garlic**: 1 clove (minced)
- **Olive oil**: 1 teaspoon
- **Vegetable broth**: 1 cup
- **Whole milk or cream**: ¼ cup
- **Salt and black pepper**: To taste
- **Optional garnish**: Fresh thyme sprig

Instructions

1. **Sauté Aromatics**: Heat **olive oil** in a pot over medium heat. Add **onion** and **garlic**, and cook for 3 minutes.
2. **Cook Vegetables**: Add **Brussels sprouts** and **potatoes**, cooking for 5 minutes.
3. **Simmer the Chowder**: Add **vegetable broth** and simmer for 15 minutes until the vegetables are tender.
4. **Blend and Add Cream**: Blend the soup partially for a creamy texture. Stir in **milk or cream** and season with **salt** and **pepper**. Garnish with fresh thyme.

Brussels Sprouts and Bacon Broth

Serves: 1 | Prep Time: 10 mins | Cook Time: 20 mins

Ingredients

- **Brussels sprouts**: ½ cup (halved)
- **Bacon**: 1 slice (chopped)
- **Onion**: ¼ medium (chopped)
- **Garlic**: 1 clove (minced)
- **Vegetable broth**: 1¼ cups
- **Salt and black pepper**: To taste
- **Optional garnish**: Crumbled bacon

Instructions

1. **Cook the Bacon**: In a pot, cook **bacon** over medium heat until crispy. Remove and set aside.
2. **Sauté the Vegetables**: In the bacon drippings, sauté **onion**, **garlic**, and **Brussels sprouts** for 5 minutes.
3. **Simmer the Broth**: Add **vegetable broth** and simmer for 10 minutes.
4. **Season and Serve**: Adjust seasoning with **salt** and **pepper**. Garnish with crumbled bacon.

Brussels Sprouts and Sweet Potato Soup

Serves: 1 | Prep Time: 10 mins | Cook Time: 25 mins

Ingredients

- **Brussels sprouts**: ½ cup (halved)
- **Sweet potato**: ½ cup (cubed)
- **Garlic**: 1 clove (minced)
- **Onion**: ¼ medium (chopped)
- **Olive oil**: 1 teaspoon
- **Vegetable broth**: 1¼ cups
- **Ground cinnamon**: ¼ teaspoon
- **Salt and black pepper**: To taste
- **Optional garnish**: Fresh parsley

Instructions

1. **Sauté Aromatics**: Heat **olive oil** in a pot over medium heat. Add **onion**, **garlic**, and **cinnamon**, cooking for 2–3 minutes.
2. **Cook Vegetables**: Add **Brussels sprouts** and **sweet potato**, stirring well. Cook for 5 minutes.
3. **Simmer the Soup**: Add **vegetable broth** and simmer for 15–20 minutes until the vegetables are tender.
4. **Blend and Serve**: Blend the soup until smooth. Season with **salt** and **pepper**. Garnish with fresh parsley.

Benefits of Brussels Sprout Soups

Benefit	Why It's Great
Rich in Vitamin K	Brussels sprouts are high in vitamin K, which supports bone health and helps with proper blood clotting during fall.
Boosts Immune Health	Packed with vitamin C and antioxidants, Brussels sprouts help strengthen the immune system and fight off seasonal colds.
Supports Digestion	High in fiber, Brussels sprouts aid digestion and help maintain gut health, perfect for a fall detox.
Anti-Inflammatory	Brussels sprouts contain compounds that help reduce inflammation, making them beneficial for overall health during cooler months.
Rich in Antioxidants	Full of antioxidants, they help protect the body from oxidative stress and free radical damage.

Tip: Add roasted Brussels sprouts or crispy bacon bits for extra texture and flavor in your soup!

Tips for Seasonal Cooking

Ingredient Spotlight: Choosing Fresh Produce

Seasonal cooking begins with understanding how to select the best ingredients for their peak freshness, flavor, and nutritional value. Here's a detailed guide to help you make informed choices and substitutions when ingredients are unavailable.

The Benefits of Seasonal Cooking

Aspect	Why It Matters
Enhanced Flavor	Produce harvested at peak ripeness offers superior taste and natural sweetness.
Nutritional Value	Seasonal ingredients are fresher, retaining more vitamins and minerals.
Cost Efficiency	Seasonal items are often more affordable due to local abundance and reduced transport costs.
Sustainability	Supporting local farms reduces the carbon footprint of shipping produce.

Choosing Fresh Produce

Selecting quality ingredients is crucial for exceptional meals. Use these cues to identify the freshest seasonal items:

Ingredient	Signs of Freshness	Season
Tomatoes	Bright red or vibrant color, slightly soft to the touch, and aromatic.	Summer
Apples	Firm, smooth skin without bruises or wrinkling.	Fall
Asparagus	Firm stalks, tightly closed tips, and bright green or purple color.	Spring
Pumpkins	Hard, unblemished skin and a hollow sound when tapped.	Fall
Spinach and Kale	Crisp, dark green leaves with no wilting or yellowing.	Spring, Fall
Root Vegetables	Heavy for their size, with firm, smooth skin and no soft spots.	Fall, Winter

Pro Tips for Freshness

- **Avoid Overripe Produce**: Wrinkles, dull skin, or overly soft textures often signal aging.
- **Smell the Fruit**: Aromatic fruits like melons, peaches, and berries are a sign of ripeness.
- **Weight Matters**: Heavier items like squash or root vegetables are more hydrated and flavorful.

Adapting Recipes for Off-Season Ingredients

Off-season cooking doesn't have to compromise taste. With smart substitutions, you can recreate seasonal recipes year-round.

Substitution Strategies

Seasonal Ingredient	Off-Season Substitute	Usage Tips
Fresh Tomatoes	Canned fire-roasted tomatoes	Adds depth to soups, stews, and chilis.
Fresh Herbs (Basil, Dill)	Dried herbs or jarred herb pastes	Use ⅓ the amount of dried herbs.
Zucchini or Summer Squash	Frozen zucchini slices or diced carrots	Works well in soups and stir-fries.
Sweet Corn	Frozen corn kernels	Add directly to soups, no thawing needed.
Fresh Peas	Frozen peas	Add at the end of cooking to maintain texture.
Spinach	Frozen spinach or kale	Thaw and squeeze out water before use.

Ingredient Substitution Chart

Original Ingredient	Substitute	Flavor Profile Adjustments
Fresh Strawberries	Frozen strawberries	Use in purees or desserts, slightly sweeter.
Lemon Juice	White vinegar or lime juice	Adjust sweetness in recipes accordingly.
Butternut Squash	Canned pumpkin	Adjust seasoning for a slightly sweeter taste.
Fresh Berries	Dried cranberries or raisins	Soak in water for plumpness if needed.

Storing and Freezing for Convenience

Proper storage and freezing can extend the life of fresh ingredients, helping you enjoy seasonal flavors anytime.

Storage Guidelines

Ingredient	Storage Method	Shelf Life
Leafy Greens	Wrap in a damp paper towel and place in a sealed bag in the fridge.	3–5 days
Root Vegetables	Store in a cool, dark, and dry place away from onions.	1–3 weeks
Fresh Herbs	Place upright in a glass of water, like a bouquet, and loosely cover with plastic.	5–7 days
Cooked Soups/Stews	Refrigerate in airtight containers.	3–4 days (or freeze)

Freezing Techniques

1. **Blended Soups**: Avoid freezing soups with dairy; add cream after reheating to maintain texture.
2. **Chunky Soups and Stews**: Cool completely, then portion into airtight containers or freezer bags for easy storage.
3. **Individual Portions**: Freeze soups in ice cube trays for quick reheating of small servings.

Type of Dish	Best Freezing Method	Thawing Tips
Vegetable Soups	Freeze flat in zip-top bags to save space.	Thaw in the fridge overnight.
Chilis and Stews	Store in rigid containers, leaving space for expansion.	Reheat on low heat, stirring often.
Cream Soups	Freeze without dairy; add after reheating.	Heat gently to avoid curdling.

Pro Tips for Freezing and Thawing

- **Labeling**: Always label containers with the recipe name and freezing date.
- **Flash-Freezing**: For ingredients like herbs, spread them on a tray and freeze before transferring to bags to avoid clumping.
- **Quick Thawing**: For last-minute use, place frozen soups in a sealed bag and submerge in warm water.

Visual Seasonal Ingredient Replacement Guide

Here's a handy table to quickly identify alternatives:

Seasonal Recipe Ingredient	Alternative	When to Use
Fresh Basil (Spring)	Pesto sauce or dried basil	Pairs well with pasta dishes and soups.
Fresh Pumpkin (Fall)	Canned pumpkin puree	Ideal for baked goods and creamy soups.
Bell Peppers (Summer)	Roasted jarred peppers	Use in stews or as toppings for grains.
Fresh Berries (Summer)	Frozen mixed berries	Perfect for smoothies and dessert sauces.

BONUS

Scan this QR Code and Download your Bonus with Extra Seasonal Recipes here!

Note: it's obviously completely free. If ads pops up simply close them. In case you have problems accessing it or simply prefer we send you the pdf file email us at contactmebonus@gmail.com

Conclusion

Soup isn't just food; it's a story in a bowl. Every spoonful tells a tale of tradition, comfort, and creativity. Through this cookbook, we've explored the incredible diversity of soups—from creamy classics to broths brimming with bold spices, hearty stews that feel like a warm hug, and refreshing bowls perfect for sunny days.

Whether you've discovered a new family favorite or found joy in perfecting the basics, this collection is here to remind you that soup-making is as much about the journey as it is about the destination. It's about the gentle simmer of flavors, the aroma that fills your kitchen, and the satisfaction of sharing something wholesome with the people you care about.

So, as you close this book, remember that the magic of soup lies in its adaptability. Let these recipes inspire you to experiment, to tweak, and to make each bowl uniquely your own. After all, the best soups are made with a pinch of creativity, a dash of love, and a whole lot of heart.

Here's to many more bowls of deliciousness ahead. Happy cooking!

Made in the USA
Monee, IL
20 December 2024

74819331R00066